CREATING
RITUALS

A New Way
of Healing
for Everyday Life

Rev. Jim Clarke, PhD

Paulist Press
New York / Mahwah, NJ

Cover design by Sharyn Banks
Book design by Lynn Else

Library of Congress Cataloging-in-Publication Data

Clarke, Jim (James J.)
    Creating rituals : a new way of healing for everyday life / Jim Clarke.
        p. cm.
    Includes bibliographical references (p.   ).
    ISBN 978-0-8091-4716-8 (alk. paper)
    1. Spiritual healing. 2. Ritual. I. Title.
    BT732.5.C58 2011
    234'.131—dc22

                                                        2010042904

Published by Paulist Press
997 Macarthur Boulevard
Mahwah, New Jersey 07430

www.paulistpress.com

Printed and bound in the
United States of America

Contents

In memory of my parents, Bill and Trudy Clarke,
who gave me the material to shape my life.
I am grateful that they taught me the necessity of creating
rituals to negotiate the many transitions along
my journey from childhood to maturity.

1

Transformation:
It Really Can Happen

SEVERAL YEARS AGO, Claudia, a client of mine, lost her husband to cancer. It had been a long and loving marriage of twenty-five years, but had been fraught with suffering in the area of sexuality. Two years before David's death, he had disclosed to her his homosexuality—perhaps not a surprise to her, but a profound shock nevertheless. His death was sudden when it came, and he left behind journals in which he had reflected on his terrible struggles. This was deeply painful reading for Claudia, leaving her in a state of emotional chaos. Anger, grief, resentment, and regrets tumbled in with feelings of compassion, love, and a deep sense of loss and bewilderment. A year after his death, she was still paralyzed by this complex of contradictory feelings and seemed unable to move forward at all.

I suggested a ritual that might lead her out of the emotional hellhole in which she felt trapped. She agreed immediately, more out of hope than expectation of success; nothing else had seemed to help.

The first step was a discussion of her emotional impasse and the desire she had to resume her life. We explored different symbols that might give expression to the confusion and chaos in her feeling world. We decided upon the appropriate dramatic action and chose the setting.

We drove to the ocean and lit a small fire near the water's edge. As I sat at a distance, supportive but not participating, Claudia took the journals and intentionally and reverently, page by page, tore them into small pieces and dropped them into the flames. As Claudia worked, she quietly spoke of her love for David, of their sufferings, of his painful struggles, of their precious memories, and of their children, born of their love. As day faded into dusk and dimmed into twilight, the flames consumed their twenty-five-year story, and Claudia felt and spoke of the liberation of her spirit. In her reverent letting-go, she understood his freeing of her. As darkness fell, she gathered up the ashes and gently consigned them to the ocean.

The effects of this ritual were profound and lasting. The liberation of Claudia's spirit enabled her to embark on a new and fulfilling life, embracing new relationships while lovingly integrating her history. She was able to recognize and accept her past in all its dimensions, and to integrate the fullness of her experience into her new life.

Rituals can change our lives. When we are experiencing ourselves as emotionally stuck, rituals can shift our focus and act as catapults to launch us forward in life. When we are feeling lonely, isolated, or disconnected from our deepest, truest self, rituals can reconnect us. When we're feeling out of control, rituals can contain the chaos and actively direct the situation toward a resolution.

Are you trapped in fear or insecurity? Rituals can empower you. Are you dissatisfied with your spiritual life, feeling empty, meaningless, with no sense of direction? Rituals can transform the way you pray, worship, and celebrate. Sound too good to be true?

Ritual making is not a panacea for all our human ills or a magic pill for our life's pain. Rather, it is an ancient, traditional way of honoring human reality, using the language of the soul. Unfortunately, in our postmodern society, we have lost our deep connection to the soul and have forgotten its language. In our rational, scientific age, we have come to distrust the world of the imagination, and have failed to make use of its many gifts. The soul is the place of deep emotions, attachments, history, art, music, dreams, imagination, silence, and memories. Therefore, the human soul "reads" reality from a different perspective. The soul cannot tell the difference between ritual and reality, as both are seen as metaphorical. As far back as 70,000 years ago, ancient peoples understood this mysterious truth, and used ritual as a means of expressing their deepest human longings. This was their way of dealing with loss, transition, and emotional pain.

Claudia's ritual worked for her because she found an embodied language that adequately expressed her conflicted feelings, while at the same time releasing the hold that these emotions had on her. In ritual space, she let go of the past, so that she could fully live in the present. Claudia acted out her own "death" to the past, thus "rising" in the present moment.

I am reminded of the story recounted by Luke in his Gospel (8:43–48), of a woman who, for twelve years, had suffered a debilitating hemorrhage. Her grief was not only for her body, but also for her spirit; under Jewish law, she was isolated from communal life. She carried this open wound, this loss of life, until the day she ritually encountered her own unique source of healing in her meeting and action with Jesus. That first-century Palestinian woman's preparatory work of visiting doctors, searching, and praying was necessary as she moved toward that moment of healing. Her process culminated in her ritual action of intentionally and reverently touching Jesus' garment, while silently voicing her deepest desire for healing. Claudia's preparatory work of speaking with one or two close friends, journaling, praying, and paying attention to her tears and pain was likewise necessary toward her healing, but the final piece of the drama was lacking. Her ritual was the consummation of all that had gone before. It is good to remind ourselves that for both of these women, separated by centuries, God was the author of the healing that took place.

As Christians, we claim that we are a people of word and sacrament, story and ritual, but often we view this reality solely as a singular sanctuary or ecclesial event, belonging to the exclusive domain of a few chosen liturgical leaders, rather than a daily lived reality. I believe that without regularly integrating story and ritual into our daily lives, our potential for happiness is significantly lessened.

A ritual is a symbolic action or series of actions, accompanied by meaningful words that encapsulate and express the cultural and personal values of the participants. A ritual gives body to the inner reality of the participants. This reality is then given power or affirmation by the presence of the witnessing community.

In light of the above, let's look at Claudia's ritual practice and explore why it worked so well. In her own way, Claudia initially had tried to "fix" her complex grief by putting it out of her mind, but this didn't work because an unexpressed truth keeps returning until it is honorably acknowledged.

The ritual, with all its elements in place, honored the needs of her soul for the following reasons:

- She acknowledged the facts of the relationship with her husband (e.g., their love, her sense of betrayal, death).
- She welcomed all the dark, conflicted feelings about their relationship and about him.
- She allowed these feelings to simmer for a while, paying attention to her tears and pain.

- She journaled, prayed, and spoke to one or two intimate friends.
- She chose a meaningful place and time for the ritual: beside the ocean's edge at dusk. For her, the ocean symbolized the chaos of her soul and yet was a place she loved. Underneath the turbulent surface, she knew, was a deep calm, to which she aspired.
- She used a multivocal symbol that honored the oppositional tendencies within her: fire and water.
- She mindfully created a dramatic embodied action that expressed her grief. Claudia gently, but very purposefully, tore the pages of her husband's journal while speaking words of tenderness, compassion, and forgiveness. Dropping the torn pages into the fire was a symbol of the Earth receiving and containing her pain, transforming it into ashes—ashes of grief she had already tasted in her mouth. The casting of the ashes into the ocean dissolved the last vestiges of her pain and carried it to the depths.
- My presence, as witness, affirmed her and honored her pain.

Across time and space, Claudia clearly acknowledged her past pain and created a new imaginal reality, just as did the biblical woman with the hemorrhage. After celebrating this ritual, Claudia experienced an immediate and powerful transformation. In her own words, "A black cloud lifted within a week and never returned." She received a completely new perspective and understanding of her grief. She now saw with new eyes, experiencing deep compassion, peace, and contentment. Once Claudia entered into this profound encounter with the real wound of her soul, using its own language, the ritual released its power to heal, and opened up for her a more expansive view of her life—we might even call it the divine view.

Rituals are meant to be unique for each person, group, or situation. Certainly, one size does not fit all. This particular ritual worked its magic of transformation because Claudia tailored the elements of good ritual to her situation—not the other way around. Ritual is always in the service of the participants.

The vicissitudes of life touch each one of us and our loved ones in different ways. None of us emerges unscathed, untroubled by life's difficulties. Divorce, death of loved ones, midlife crises, betrayal, health setbacks, accidents, and developmental changes are only a few of the challenges that we might face on our life's journey. I'm sure that you can add other life struggles to the list.

What this book will teach you is how to successfully celebrate rituals for all of life's transitions, both joyful and painful, including the inevitable encounters with life's endings. At some level, ritual is always about movement from one "place" to another. Think of this book as a guidebook for negotiating the twists and turns of the soul's life journey.

Questions for Personal Reflection:

- What negative events, painful feelings, or disturbing experiences are lingering in the shadows of my heart and mind, needing release?
- Are there particular symbols that encapsulate or summarize my feelings about these events at this time?

- What words need to be spoken aloud about these events or experiences?

Questions for Parish Leaders:

- In what areas of our parishioners' lives might rituals be helpful? What are our parishioners' joys, transitions, and losses?
- What are the possibilities for individuals and for groups within the parish?
- How might the principles of good ritual be applied to the celebration of sacraments in the parish?
- Is there also a place for ritual in the parish sacramental programs, which tend to have a more informal focus?

Tips for Parish Leaders:

- As this is a largely unexplored field in parish life, I suggest that the parish staff team read this book together and discuss its implications for improving the ritual life of the parish. Since the priest will most often be the ritual leader, it is important that he is part of this process.
- We tend to focus on the big occasions—mostly sacramental—but after reading this book you will realize there are many wonderful moments in people's lives that can be deepened and transformed by ritual.

2

Bringing Up Baby: Giving Them Wings to Fly

LIFE TRANSITIONS ARE like doorways, inviting the individual or group to pass over into another space. Rituals are like keys that unlock these doors and facilitate crossing the thresholds. The crossing-over is actually powered by the ritual event. Ritual gives context to our place in the mystery of the cosmos—it frames the meaning of a person's present situation and addresses the desire to understand the paradox of reality, especially the wounding nature of life. Ritual can offer healing, reconciliation, and balm to life's painful struggles. An illustration from my childhood might provide an insight into my own understanding of what is at the heart of ritual practice.

When I was nine years old, my parents sent me to a local college for summer swimming lessons. In order to enter the pool, I had to go into the locker room and undress. It embarrassed me to have to appear almost naked in front of the older boys and adults. On leaving the locker room, in my swimming trunks, I then had to walk through a short passage where the showers were, a prerequisite for entering the pool. Going through these showers—walking through powerful jets of water that assaulted my body to prepare me to go swimming in the deep—was scary. Dripping wet, I exited into the pool area and was escorted to one of three diving boards, where I was ordered to jump into the deep end of the pool. One look at the depth of the pool sent shudders through my whole body, and my fear was exacerbated by the loud command of the lifeguard to jump immediately. But I did it, plunging into the depths of the pool. I surfaced with great focus and clarity. Although I had no prior experience of being in deep water, I was told to swim toward a pole held by a lifeguard standing at the edge of the pool. Fearful but energized, I dog paddled furiously to the pole. I experienced exhilaration, realizing that I had done it and could do it again. Thus began my swimming lesson. Getting out of the pool, I knew that I was ready for the next time.

For me, this story is a metaphor for understanding the nature and function of ritual. The locker room is the place of ritual preparation—the talking, the discussing, the planning. It is where we divest ourselves of what is not needed to enter a deeper experience of our humanity and clarify what we are about, in order to be ready for a transformative experience. It is in this anteroom of ritual that we might face the emotional embarrassment of nakedness in having to name truthfully our deepest urges and feelings. The shower passageway is a metaphor for the ritual experience: the transhistorical time, the transgeographical place, where all these emotions can be named, cleansed, purified, held up, and honored in all their polarities. In this liminal space we sense intuitively that this is an experience beyond language, beyond explanation. It is a leap into the unknown, the place of imagination or desire.

Each person has a unique internal reality and experience in ritual. Often we cannot articulate it, but it is an experience of embodied knowing in which the past, the present, and the future are held, sustained, and expressed in this liminal space. Many people, unable to find appropriate words for what they have experienced, simply say "I'm not the same" or "life is different." It is here, in this chamber of ritual, that we can engage the darkness of our fear and the unclaimed parts of our interior life. Words are subservient to the dramatic ritual action.

Symbols are essential components of ritual, because they bridge the historical and the geographical, and hold power and energy simultaneously. A young woman friend of mine told me some time ago of the experience of her daughter's first communion. The event and the preparation for it had been filled with the usual excitement and joy—a new dress purchased, the liturgical participation rehearsed, the party planned. But there was something special here; the mother had carefully preserved her own first communion veil, and her little girl was wearing it for her special day. As this woman sat in the eucharistic assembly, watching with pride and joy, she became aware of being profoundly moved. There was more than a liturgical rite; there was more than a mother's pride in a beautiful daughter. A larger drama was unfolding. What was happening here? Through the symbol of the veil, she stepped into another world in which she could only vaguely grasp what was unfolding, but it held her in its power, and through her tears she "saw" the memory of a past event merge with the pride of the present moment and future hope for her daughter. Time and place merged in an emotional congruence of tremendous proportion that she herself was unable to explain.

For some, ritual is a kind of shock or reawakening to a primordial form of expression of an already present truth. The pool at my local college can be seen as a metaphor for the new, deeper reality that is to come, into which one is about to plunge. Ritual empowers and strengthens us to dive into the depths of the reality of life, where often we will face an uncertain future. Ritual reminds us that we have passed through into something new, something profoundly meaningful. We are no longer the same.

The unfolding of each person's unique humanity proceeds through discernible stages, beginning with conception and continuing through death. Along the way, we must be faithful at all costs to the needs of our soul. To violate this aspect of our own mysterious human reality is to go against the very nature of God, as well as against our own nature as beloved sons and daughters of God. For those of us in the Christian tradition, events such as baptism and confirmation, expressed in the community of believers, are a response to this innate need to care for our soul. But for all of us, Christian or not, there are a number of significant moments of transition to be marked, celebrated, and honored. Looking at just our first twenty-five years, these might include birth, the first day of school, puberty, obtaining a driver's license, trauma (such as a major accident, health crisis, or our parents' divorce), graduation from different levels of academic achievement, leaving home to live independently, bringing home a baby for the first time. You can undoubtedly name more of your own.

Life-cycle changes, especially within family structures, are enormously complicated affairs and can be fraught with conflicting emotions. For this reason, many cultures have created ritual celebrations to guide their people through these transitions. Welcoming a baby home is a perfect opportunity to create a ritual for the child and to honor the changes that will take place in the family structure and dynamics. In this case, the ritual can serve as an embodied reminder that things will indeed be different for everyone concerned. Participation by all members of the family household is key to the success of such an acceptance ritual. This might be especially pertinent, for example, when welcoming a foster child or a newly adopted child into the family. There is a clear need here for a communication dynamic that assists in the unpacking of any conflicted feelings and beliefs within the original family structure.

The first day of school represents a change of mythic proportions. At first glance, this event appears rather modest in the overall context of a person's life. Let's look carefully, however, at what this change implies. Parents hand over the larger part of the education and socialization of their child to an institution. This signifies that the parents are stepping aside and inviting the larger community into the formation of this little person's life. It is now a collaborative effort, not limited to the home environment. For the child's part, he or she will be introduced to a larger community of friends and acquaintances that will, for better or worse, influence his or her values and happiness. He or she will never be the same again. Surely, this event deserves recognition and celebration!

What symbol(s) might be chosen to represent the underlying feelings on the part of the participants in the event? What words need expression? What dramatic action could enhance this moment of transition for the child and the family? Who should assist in the planning and participate in the ritual event? When and in what setting ought this ritual to occur? It might be exciting to think about the possibilities for your family or extended family.

There are numerous possibilities for ritual expression of movements within adolescence, even before the progression to adulthood is addressed. One thinks of the time of a girl's first period or a boy's first shave. A teenager learning to drive a car or beginning his or her first regularly paying job is a wonderful moment of clarity about personal and social responsibility. I remember one of my younger brothers having a high-school driving instructor who saw the possibility to reframe this time into a transformative moment for his students by incorporating driving instruction into the larger narrative of life. He drew parallels between driving a vehicle on a state highway and moving along the highway of life. His preparatory questions about "how do you want to get to your destination," "what do you need to be mindful of," "which way will you take," and "who will accompany you" formed part of the discussion before each lesson. At the conclusion of the final lesson, he then ritually expressed the transitional moment by handing the car keys to the student, with the words: "These are the keys to your life." These performative words highlighted the dramatic action and meaning of the handing over of the keys. His students never forgot this experience; I know my brother never did. This is the mark of effective ritual: Transformation took place, as measured by the participants' response and interior affirmation.

Family and communal rituals accompanying graduation ceremonies can be most empowering, not only for the individual, but also for the family, and often for the institution. Joining the private and public aspects of the various stages of academic development through ritual expression often strengthens communal relationships. Ritual can bridge the paradoxical tension between the need for individual freedom on the one hand and social coherence on the other. This seems to be particularly so in the case of the children of immigrants graduating from college. Their whole college experience has propelled them more urgently into discovering their identity as bicultural persons, but there exists at the same time the pull of the cohesion of the family unit. The values of the two different communities often conflict. This marker moment invites ritual. The celebration of their academic success is not only for themselves but also for the whole family as well as the college community. I have experienced this firsthand; I see in the eyes of those parents a unique sense of pride. Often, they are so moved they are speechless, their emotions welling up in tears. Here is the whole family's dream come alive in this young person's life. The possibilities for ritual symbolic expression are endless.

Perhaps I can say a word here about blended families and how they might transition into a new family identity. In my work with families, I have come to realize that the challenge of successful blending is particularly acute for the adolescent children. The establishment of a new family identity and unity cannot be rushed or forced. This is where ritual could help in getting the process started. Clearly, discussions will have taken place as the families prepare to come together, and will naturally serve as part of the preparatory work for the ritual enactment. What is the central focus around which each family revolves? Is it a love of participatory sports? Playing musical instruments? Camping and other outdoor activities? Attending concerts? Going to football games? Church involvement? It may well be that the new family faces a formidable task in making space for—and honoring—quite diverse values, interests, and passions. Thus, a family might choose to redecorate the "new" family home together, in whole or in part, and seek to integrate established family customs and traditions within new ones.

A blended family I know created a large wall hanging for their living room that depicted the various interests and passions of all the members of the two families. It made a wonderful conversation piece, not only for them, but also for visitors and friends. These family actions can be the basis for developing rituals, while the words are secondary or supportive of the dramatic action. Anthropologist Victor Turner saw ritual as offering a cathartic release of emotional tension as well as giving form to conflicts and the dominant values that hold the group together. This is done through the ritual dramatization of the actual situation. The creation and the displaying of the wall hanging constituted a private and public enactment of their commitment to their joint future, enriched by the combined talents and gifts of all of them. The past, the present, and the future came together in this ritualization.

Some questions that might assist you in beginning to address the ritual needs of your own blended family are: What issues are unique to your family? Do you need to integrate a bicultural or biracial family? Are the children the same age, or are there different generations of children? Will the children change their last name as well? How are the children to be involved in the wedding ceremony or transition into a new home? What symbols can be used for each member of the family to express his or her own conflicted emotions? What words need to be spoken publicly by each person? Is there a particular action that can adequately portray the common desire for family unity and happiness? When and where should this ritual take place?

Leaving home for the first time can be a memorable and meaningful experience for a young person when planned with purpose and direction. Departure for college or marriage can be ritually honored in a deeply affirming manner that liberates the young person into his or her own adulthood. I will never forget the response of my family when I announced my decision to transfer from a local community college to St. John's Seminary College. This was a particularly momentous transition moment because the implication—indeed, the intention—was that I would be entering the priesthood and leaving them in a way that was different and unique. They were genuinely happy for me, but they also expressed their deep sadness at my leaving. I, too, was conflicted. I felt fearful, sad, and filled with self-doubt in the face of this momentous decision. We discussed these complex emotional responses and decided to honor them within the context of a blessing ritual in which the whole family participated. One by one, they laid their hands on me and blessed me in their own words. Their faith in me, their encouragement of me, and their unconditional love for me all flowed through that touch. This deeply affirming memory continued to sustain me throughout the years of my seminary training, and to this day, deep inside of me, the experience and memory of that transitional moment of blessing hold me tenderly and firmly in their grasp. In a very real way, this ritual, transformative as it was, powered my movement forward into my new life and beyond.

I found in my story of ritual sending forth echoes of other, more ancient stories from the Scriptures, in particular the account of the commissioning of Paul and Barnabas by the Christian community at Antioch (Acts 13:1–3). Guided by the Spirit, the community set apart Paul and Barnabas and laid hands on them, praying words of love and encouragement, and blessing them as they left for the next stage in their journey and mission. When we explore the Scriptures with new eyes, it becomes apparent that our ancestors in faith possessed a deep intuitive sense of the importance of ritual.

Ritual work joins word, symbol, and action together in one fluent expression of interior desire. This, of course, is the foundational principle of sacramental celebration in the Christian tradition. Formed and shaped in advance, in a reflective process, the spoken word accompanies and illuminates the symbolic expression. It serves to crystallize the message, bringing it alive in a more profound way, in the soul of the participant. An important caution: A respectful balance needs to be maintained between word and action, because frequently the verbal component can be used to replace or overpower the dramatic action that is at the heart of the ritual. The symbols used must also be accorded their own integrity. Together, within the ritual, those symbols and the dramatic action strengthen and deepen the memory of the words expressed. To enter into and to live the symbolic and the imaginal is to live a genuinely religious life.

Questions for Personal Reflection:

- What transitional moments in the lives of your children (or nieces and nephews) present themselves to you and your family as opportunities for ritual acknowledgment and expression?
- What dramatic action within a planned ritual experience might adequately express your interior disposition in relation to one of these transition moments?
- Have you noticed the many ritual actions mentioned in both the Hebrew and Christian Scriptures? Can you identify the transitions that were being marked?

Questions for Parish Leaders:

- Through what channels do you, as a parish leader, have the opportunity to nurture and enhance the lives of the children of the parish?
- If the primary channels are the schools and religious education programs, how can you work with teachers and students to introduce this new dimension of catechesis?
- Do the symbols presently in use in parish liturgical life, especially in sacramental celebrations, reflect the realities of the families in your parish?
- In what ways could the parish ritually honor and support the transitional events that perme-

ate childhood, adolescence, and young adulthood?

Tips for Parish Leaders:

- Example is a powerful teacher in the area of good ritual. Working with teachers and catechists to develop effective classroom rituals might be a good way to begin to catch the attention of parents.
- Take the opportunity in prayer groups, Bible study groups, and other small parish interest groups to introduce this concept. Work with the presenting issues, responding to the real-life situations of families, rather than imposing a new practice from outside.
- From a pastoral perspective, you might consider using ritual as a means of affirming, blessing, or healing family relationships.

3

Adolescence to Adulthood: One Giant Leap for Humankind

THE HUMAN LIFE cycle necessarily involves times of transition. Each of us must negotiate these crossings. Over the centuries, cultures and societies have supported these moments through communal rituals and ceremonies. In postmodern times, however, this wisdom has been lost, and, with it, the ability for many to negotiate these crucial transitions in a healthy way. Nowhere is this more evident than in the movement from adolescence to adulthood. Perhaps the most important of our ancestors' communal rituals were traditional initiation rites. This is not surprising; we are "hardwired" for initiation, and it will happen one way or another. Our ancestors knew this, and created ways to assist and support the passage from dependent child to independent adult. We need hardly say that contemporary society is in real need of such a mechanism, given that our children are catapulted earlier and earlier into an adulthood for which they are, in most cases, ill-prepared.

This leaves the adolescent in a quandary, torn between family expectations, media hype, and conflicting cultural values. Adolescence can be a dangerous time when the proper guidance of elders is absent. In addition to our cultural weaknesses of individualism, materialism, militarism, and even self-gratification, there are other social and psychological problems in our culture that contribute to this danger. Psychologists John Sanford and George Lough have identified five of these issues as significant.

First, we have no guide for the phenomenon of prolonged adolescence that has developed in Western culture, particularly in North America. As a result, greater stress is placed on the parent/adolescent relationship. There is no healthy communal support for growing through adolescence. For this reason, the adolescent undergoes, over a number of years, unnecessary struggles with his/her identity and perception of self.

Second, our society tends to withhold from our young people the opportunity to assume real responsibility or mature work that would assist them in stabilizing their ego. Before the age of eighteen, mostly gone are authentic opportunities for apprenticeship, an early start in a career, or public service. This inhibits the maturation process of large numbers of adolescents, serves to prolong their childishness, and reinforces a sense of irresponsibility.

Third, North American culture lacks real spiritual depth—the veneer of religiosity barely covers a sea of fear, anxiety, and angry violence. Religiosity, whether expressed in liturgical rites, Scripture quotes, entertaining music, emotional testimonies, or repetitive prayer forms, essentially offers no real transformation of the individual that is visibly expressed in society. The individual ego seeks to be assuaged and strengthened by the group ego. Scripture, doctrine, and tradition are then used as proof that one is correct, not changed or transformed. Rare is the person able to grow in awareness or to experience the mystical teaching of his/her religious group. Whatever one's belief system, the bottom line appears to the trained observer to be that American civic religion is the religion of the times. American civic religion is mostly about material progress and success, and fails to offer the young person encouragement to turn inward for silent reflection or contemplation. Thrill seeking and the quest for ecstatic experience are, in reality, the expressions of the urge of the psyche for wholeness.

Fourth, our culture fails to provide people with safe, legitimate means of spiritual experience. As a result, many turn to thrill seeking, drugs, and alcohol for altered states of consciousness. Historically, this natural need for ecstatic experiences had been filled by religion. Today, it is filled by profane elements in society. We see this most clearly in the increasing popularity of the adrenaline rush of extreme sports, mind-altering experiences of alternative forms of music, entertainment excesses, and an increase in violent sports and addictive/compulsive behaviors.

Fifth, our culture presents a false or incomplete image of what it means to be an adult. We live by the way we construct our worldview, and the dominant culture's emphasis on crude, macho masculinity as status symbol often puts adolescents at risk in their drinking, dating, and driving behavior (Sanford and Lough, 48–50). To this observation, I would add the sexualized model of femininity thrust upon young girls by the media and by marketing professionals. Whether or not you agree with this cultural commentary in its entirety, it is undeniable that our adolescents are subjected to enormously unhealthy influences and pressures.

Without a cultural setting and sacred container for meaningful initiatory pathways, young people will seek to do it themselves—consciously or unconsciously. The archetype of wholeness or individuation draws people forward on their lifelong journey. In our culture, religious ceremonies such as confirmation or bar mitzvah have attempted to fill this void, with varying degrees of success. Certainly, they function as religious initiation events within the Christian and Jewish traditions, respectively, but often these ceremonies have been adapted to the point where they are no longer effective as authentic initiation rites in the context of the development of the person. Part of the reason for this failure is that only one of the classic phases of initiation is present—that of incorporation. There is no separation from family or community, nor is there any element of the physically challenging "trials" that often accompany initiation in traditional social groups. Hence, there is no bridging of opposites or engagement with the shadow—that is, the dark, unknown, unnamed elements of reality. I will speak more on this aspect of ritual later. Suffice to say there is no transformative element in these celebrations.

Cultural changes have had an impact on many religious practices and rituals. In the early centuries of Christianity, liturgical celebrations were interactive rituals that demanded the involvement of the participants. These rituals have devolved into ceremonies, with participants experiencing no real change in themselves because of their attendance. Ceremony honors what has taken place with no real expectation for change. Ritual, on the other hand, is all about transformation and transitioning into something new. "Ritual is transformative, ceremony confirmatory" (Turner, *The Ritual Process*, 6). At best then, these religious activities are pleasant ceremonies, not meaningful rituals. The status of the individual has not really changed. Life continues in pretty much the same vein as before.

Meaningful ritual appeals to the senses in startling ways because it encompasses body, soul, thought, and action. When ritual is mindfully undertaken and culturally constructed, it gives the participants a transforming experience of the present moment. Think of some of the ancient Christian traditions, now lost: the spoonful of salt given to the baptized as a symbol of welcome and preservation of relationship with the community; the slap to the side of the face given by the bishop to the newly confirmed as a sign of peace; the stages of entrance into the church, marked by rites of initiation that involved fasting, prayer, lengthy instructions, and full immersion in water. Even more dramatic, the Order of Penitents, in which sackcloth-clad sinners publicly fasted, gave alms, and prayed for forgiveness, all the while begging the faithful, from outside the assembly, to join them in interceding for their forgiveness. What has been sacrificed in abandoning these embodied rituals is the active participation of the whole person in the liturgical experience. Today, the body is ignored, leaving the focus to the intellectual engagement in the liturgy. The body then rebels with discomfort and agitation, while the intellect responds with distractions, doubts, or temptations. Is it any surprise, then, that in some quarters of the Christian Church, there is a yearning to return to some of these ancient penitential or devotional practices as a means of engaging the whole person?

How can we retrieve this wisdom of the past for our adolescents and apply it in our contemporary society? I am convinced that we need to develop and use good ritual in the service of the initiation process.

What is initiation? It is an experience of one's personal power in relationship to others. This process assists a person in answering the perennial questions of who am I in relationship to others, to the cosmos, to God? Where do I fit? What are my limitations? What is my mission in life? This is profound spiritual work.

Let me tell you the story of one boy's ritual initiation.

Some years ago, I suggested to my eight brothers the idea of an annual father/son weekend. I would facilitate the weekends as a means of deepening the relationships between them and their sons, in a setting that would be fun, exciting, but also challenging to the boys as they grew into adolescence and manhood. They eagerly accepted, and we have been gathering for these camping weekends for more than fifteen years. The boys are invited to attend as they reach an age at which their own father believes they are sufficiently mature to participate. This varies with the individual. Throughout the weekend, we play games, engage in meaningful teaching and dialogue with the boys, and undertake a lengthy hike, backpacking trip, or kayak adventure. We use these outdoor activities as a metaphor for life: Themes such as adequate preparation and training, how to persevere for the long haul, keeping the end goal in focus, and so on, give us a structure for imparting the big lessons of life. I share some traditional stories of masculine development with the boys and create lively discussion. The boys enter eagerly into this process, and ultimately all of this is integrated into the rituals that take place during the two days.

One year, the final ritual of the weekend proved transformative for all of us. It took the form of an initiation for the boys, but its power was such that none of us has ever forgotten it. On this occasion, my father was also present; this added an even deeper dimension for the boys. This ritual was repeated separately for each boy in turn.

I invited my father and my eight brothers to form two lines facing each other. The boys waited some distance away, unsure of what was going to take place. The father of the boy participating in the exercise at any one time stayed with the other boys, away from the action. I will use my nephew Andrew's experience in this story. Andrew came and stood first before his grandfather, and, as instructed, looked him in the eye, as his grandfather affirmed him in his schoolwork, his athletic prowess, and his musical talents. Next, Andrew turned and faced his Uncle Tony, who named his communication skills and friendliness as commendable qualities. His Uncle Daniel spoke of Andrew's playfulness and good humor. On down the lines Andrew went, back and forth, collecting each affirmation as if it were treasure—which indeed it was.

When this process finished, I brought his father, John, back into the group. John, while knowing the general category of our affirmations, nevertheless knew nothing of what we had said. He faced his son, looked into his eyes, and began with these memorable words: "Andrew, you are the boy I always dreamed of having." Tears welled up in Andrew's eyes; he burst into tears, oblivious to everyone around him except his father, from whom he had never heard such words of blessing. John, deeply moved, wept with his son. He then began a beautiful litany of the goodness and beauty he saw in his boy. He named everything the nine of us men had named, and more. When he finished, I stepped forward with some blessed aromatic oil, which John took and daubed on Andrew's forehead, speaking these words of blessing: "Andrew, receive these gifts that have been given to you by God, named by this community of men for the good of all." Imagine how this nine-year-old boy felt. He stood ten feet tall, aglow with this blessing from these men who loved him. I asked him to return to his cousins, standing apart, saying nothing of what had happened. His older cousin, Matthew, however, seeing Andrew's face, came running to us, calling: "Whatever you gave Andrew, I want!"

In his own eyes, Andrew was small and insignificant, but the ritual blessing of these men allowed him to view and experience himself as quite the opposite.

Rituals are laden with levels of meaning. They can be innovative but, at the same time, must appeal to tradition. What makes them transformative is competent performance on the part of the participants, as they engage the shadow element. There needs to be an extended time of preparation for the ritual event, to allow an opportunity for reflection and discussion of the ritual itself. The initiation process is an exception, in that the subject is not involved in the planning and preparation. In this way, the surprise/shock element is heightened, and the memory is imprinted more deeply in the soul of the initiate. This preparatory work provides clarity and focus, so that a few well-chosen performative words within liminal space will have the desired impact. These words are subordinate to the action; in some cases, it can even be that no words are necessary. A few potent symbols are used to express the conflicting tensions within the individual or community. The embodied action that takes place before the witnessing community effects the catharsis or transformation as the individual imaginally steps into the new reality. Thus, in the ritual of Andrew's initiation, he stepped into the new reality of his own goodness and lovability mirrored in the eyes of his uncles and grandfather. The power of the ritual derived not only from the performative words (the result of preparation and reflection), but also from the two symbols: the community gauntlet and the blessed oil, which served as the touchstones for the affirmation of Andrew.

But we were by no means finished. After we had concluded the blessing of each of the boys in this manner, I then explained to the men that there was still an important component of the ritual to be enacted. For the boys' sake, we needed to repeat this "gauntlet" experience from a negative perspective; this would serve to strengthen and protect them against the darkness of the world in which they live.

We formed our lines once more and began the second phase of the ritual. This time, I instructed the boys not to look into the eyes of the men, but just to listen to the insulting words that would fly at them. Andrew began again, but this was very different. Standing before his grandfather, he heard "You're no good. You're a loser. You don't deserve to be called a Clarke. Who do you think you are, anyway?" Then it was Uncle Tony's turn, and he insulted Andrew with a few demeaning words. Uncle Daniel pushed and jostled him, calling him names. I observed that Andrew was ready to cry, but he continued down the line, taking it all in. When his father returned, he found Andrew standing at the end of the lines, his head hung low. John stood before his son, saying "Andrew, look at me!" Andrew raised his head and heard his father say, "The words you have heard from your grandfather and uncles just now are all lies. You will hear these things as you grow up. See them for what they are—lies! The truth is what you heard from us first. You are beloved in our eyes and in the eyes of God. That is what you are to carry in your heart forever. It will serve you well and strengthen you for the challenges of life."

At this point, I stood before Andrew holding a baseball cap bearing the Nike logo. Presenting the cap to him, I asked, "Andrew, do you know the meaning of the word *Nike*?" "No," he responded. "It is the Greek word for *winner* or *victor*," I replied. "In our eyes, you will always be a winner; you will be the best kind of victor as you face with courage and wisdom the challenges that will confront you throughout your life. Receive this gift as a reminder of that truth." The whole group—uncles and grandfather—then hugged Andrew warmly and sent him back to the group of boys. We repeated this second phase of the ritual until each boy had received his cap. There was a touching footnote to this story: At the conclusion of the entire ritual, two of my brothers, both of whom have experienced many difficulties in their lives, came to me quietly and commented: "How different our lives might have been if our grandfathers and uncles had done this for us. We would never have believed the lies." Both had tears in their eyes.

Andrew's story illustrates for us the difference between ceremony and ritual. The elements of effective ritual can be contrasted with the components of ceremonies, where there is no authentic transformation. Ritual takes place in liminal (out of the usual) space and time; in ceremonial celebrations, the audience gathers together in literal (*normal*) time and space, to mark an important occasion. In the latter, somewhat comfortable environment, an excess of words and symbols wearies the audience and diffuses its attention. There is no direct experience of the symbols or bodily ways of knowing, only observation of the ceremony. While ceremonies may use some ritual elements, they do not constitute rituals in and of themselves. For example, the action component, while it may be dramatic, does not engage the shadow aspect of the audience. Nobody is disturbed; nobody is challenged.

Initiation rites help an individual, through the vehicle of ritual experience within a community, to enter the problem of human suffering with a transformed consciousness. These rites are a means of inviting individuals to see the bigger picture, to experience the divine, and to discern the patterns of reality through their own experience. Moving from belief systems to embodied knowing, initiates gradually discover the hidden meaning in their ordinary life. Initiates move from a sense of aloneness to a sense of connection with all reality, as they are invited to discover their place in life. Whether for the purpose of religious indoctrination or honoring the sacredness of each individual, initiation is about becoming correctly aligned with the universe; seeing with new eyes and being transformed. Adolescents will acquire some of this wisdom at their inception into adulthood, but the initiatory experience is solidly imprinted on their psyche and remains as a persistent reminder of these teachings throughout their lives, when they encounter the challenges of mature adulthood. The lessons will continue to instruct them at ever-deepening levels of reality.

The essence of male initiation is that the boy needs to know with absolute clarity when childhood ends and when adulthood begins, along with what society expects of him. This is a distinct movement from dependency to responsibility in the community, from self-centeredness to service of humankind. Creativity, sensitivity, groundedness, and the discovery of one's place in the cosmos are the hallmarks of successful initiation rites.

I have spoken at length about male initiation, but what about the girls? In our culture, it has to be said, there are indeed already in place a variety of *initiation rites* for males— often doubtful in value, and, in some cases, downright harmful—found mostly in places like the military (boot camp), fraternities, or gangs. However, there seems to be very little available to assist girls in their transition into healthy womanhood. It seems to me that this vacuum is often filled by the excessive display and expense involved in such events as *quinceañeras* (in American culture), debutante balls, and "princess-for-a-day" weddings. Clearly, no transformation is happening here, and there has been no deepening or movement in the interior life of the girl. No initiation into the mystery of womanhood. My own first attempt at addressing this need was less than gratifying. Flushed with success after the initiation ritual with the boys, I innocently suggested to the women of the family that perhaps they might want to consider doing something similar with the girls. They laughed and said they didn't have a problem with the girls; it was the men who needed to do something meaningful with the girls.

But the work of initiating is gender-specific. The Native Peoples recognized the importance of honoring, protecting, sharing, and celebrating the power and uniqueness of what it means to be male or female, and they knew that these mysteries could only be passed on within the genders. This is why, in traditional communities, men never initiated girls; women never initiated boys. This might grate against our modern notions of gender equality and the need to know everything about the mystery of the other, but wisdom and discipline are to be recognized here.

My hope, in writing this book, is that some women readers will take up the challenge to develop rituals for girls at various stages of adolescence. Traditionally initiation has been done by the community, not directly by the parents, as there is too much special energy between parent and child. Perhaps in contemporary society this might include adult friends, relatives, teachers, neighbors, or other adults who have a stake in the child's life. As women have a natural capacity for gathering and sharing, the possibilities in this area are exciting.

Ritual helps the individual/community hold together the tension of the opposites in life, to make new connections. In adolescents, for example, such tensions might be found in the yearning for independence, while at the same time fearing it; wanting to be *different*, while at the same time wanting to conform to group expectations. This work of ritual is mirrored in the human body in the way that both hemispheres of the brain are connected, so that both the feeling and thinking functions are activated. In the performance of embodied ritual, the individual becomes the ritual; the act becomes the reality. It is in this paradoxical opposition of thoughts and feelings that he or she is stretched out on opposing planes, only to be born anew. The reward of this interior work is a sense of integration and deep peace. It might be called *at-one-ment*. Intentionality is the key here, opening the individual to something new. For transformation is not something that we do consciously; rather it is done to us, and that's what it feels like. Transformation is unique and particular to each person and situation. Ritual specialists can design the context, but the actual transformation can occur only when the individual surrenders to the experience.

A good example of this concept is to be found in the Christian Scriptures, in the story of the paralyzed man (Luke 5:17–26). His friends carry him on a bed, a symbol of complete vulnerability. When they cannot approach Jesus through the entryway, they lower him down through the roof for healing. Jesus responds with a single ritual statement: "Friend, your sins are forgiven you." This, of course, sets off an animated discussion about Christ's identity. Because the religious leaders are unable or unwilling to enter this ritual space with Jesus, they cannot imagine another reality for the paralyzed man. To placate them, Jesus tries again, this time using a more functional vocabulary: "I say to you, stand up and take your bed and go to your home." The man, who evidently has entered this imaginal reality with Jesus, sees himself as Jesus sees him—whole and complete. To the amazement of the audience, he dramatically acts out the command, a new man. He has been transformed.

Ritual attends to the process of breaking open old consciousness. In some strange way, ritual is about death—the death of egocentricity. This process gives release to the soul, the imagination. Using the elements of story, community, space, symbol, and action, ritual creates a parallel cosmos that expands the consciousness of the participant(s). For this reason, the best forms of rituals engage all the senses of the body, creating a nonordinary consciousness.

I believe that stages of initiation are multiphased, and that they are a crucial aspect of the ongoing process of human development and transformation. The challenge is to consciously construct rituals that will achieve what the practitioners intend or claim, which is transformation, and which can ultimately serve as positive substitutes for the unconsciously compelled acts to which youths are drawn, often to their own peril.

In a pluralistic society, each initiation experience must be tailored to the needs of the individual. Rites of passage might, perhaps, occur in phases, as a series of rituals over a period of years. One man tells the story of how he helped his fifteen-year-old grandson prepare for the sacrament of confirmation. In this phase of the boy's initiation, Richard took his grandson to a secluded canyon in the Southwest where he shared a traditional myth with him. Then, after ritually blessing the boy and the sacred circle, the grandfather left him alone for several hours to contemplate his surroundings and to seek guidance. As the boy waited, he observed a hawk circling in the sky above him. Here, he knew, was the message he needed for his life. He interpreted the hawk's ability to ascend on the thermal updrafts of the wind currents as an invitation to work with reality, rather than working against the context of his life. When his time of seclusion was over, Richard and his grandson came together to discuss the day's experience. They concluded their time together with a celebratory meal, awaiting the public affirmation of the confirmation ceremony a few weeks later.

In this example, the wilderness ritual broadened and deepened the meaning significance of the religious ceremony. Both ritual and ceremony were enhanced by their juxtaposed context and placement in time.

There are eight key elements to an initiation ritual:

- the community of elders
- a dramatic embodied action
- sacred time
- sacred space
- trials
- symbols
- meaningful words
- engagement of the shadow

As I have already pointed out, the community of elders ought to be gender specific. Ritual specialists can assist in creating a meaningful embodied action. Sacred time and place always involve a removal, from one's normal surroundings and routine (for example, the wilderness, retreat house, and so on). Trials are of the sort that stretch the initiates (fasting, a challenging outdoor activity, sleeplessness) to discover their limitations. Multivocal symbols are chosen selectively to express internal truths. Meaningful or performative words are carefully chosen to summarize the symbolic action (such as, "It is finished!"). Engagement of the shadow must be done wisely and insightfully through the interactive use of words and symbols.

Experiences that have worked well with young people are Outward Bound programs, vision quests, apprentice work programs, Boy Scouts (especially working toward Eagle Scout), endurance events, and immersion experiences in other cultures or impoverished environments. Working on a service project with recognized volunteer organizations such as the Peace Corps, VISTA, state and county conservation corps, urban renewal groups, and religious organizations such as the Jesuit Volunteer Corps can provide enormously challenging but very effective rites of passage settings for transformation. Any one of these programs or experiences could be used as part of an initiation process by incorporating effective rituals that speak to the participants.

Questions for Personal Reflection:

- Life will initiate us one way or another. What events, positive or negative, initiated me into adulthood?

- How might my life and my beliefs about the world and myself have been different if I had been gifted with ritual initiation?
- Is there someone in my family/intimate circle to whom this gift could be offered?

Questions for Parish Leaders:

- How could we explore, with the women of the parish, the possibilities for an initiation rite for girls? Who would be invited? Where and when would it take place?
- How can we engage boys in an effective initiation process within the parish community? What symbols might speak to their experience? What dramatic ritual actions might catch their imagination?
- Often those presenting themselves for confirmation are looking for something more than a sacramental experience. Why not explore with catechists and teachers the possibilities for a ritual of personal (as well as communal) initiation?

Tips for Parish Leaders:

- One parish in Southern California uses the annual confirmation retreat as an opportunity to present these concepts of ritual initiation to students. They are separated by gender, and the adults take the time to lead them through experience, dialogue, and ritual enactment, to assist them in integrating the lessons of transitioning into adulthood.

- Initiation is a sensitive area, and caution needs to be exercised in ensuring that parents, in particular, understand the process being undertaken, and can feel confident in the skill and integrity of the facilitators. Education will be needed as part of the preparation process.
- Refer to the Bibliography for sources that can assist you in your planning and facilitation of ritual initiations.

4

Life Stages:
Moving Forward Baggage-Free

MIDLIFE IS THE period in male adult life when we must confront the issue of separation from our previous sense of identity. For many of us, this can be a time of moderate to severe crisis. Every aspect of life comes into question, creating an atmosphere of self-doubt and even self-recrimination. This is often, though not always, manifested by irrational behavior, mood swings, thoughts of dying or death, feelings of disillusionment about life in general or with idealized persons. The questionings and searchings of this developmental period are a normal part of the process of human growth; what compounds the problem, however, is that this reappraisal of our life activates unconscious conflicts that must be addressed. This *baggage* from previous years becomes an obstacle for further growth and change in our life.

Women's experience of midlife appears to be quite different. They mostly embody midlife passage through menopause, while men's experience is more psychological. For a man, life is about accomplishment, as identity and self-respect are often wrapped up in his career achievements. Men tend to act as though midlife is a problem that must be solved rather than a mystery to be encountered. Women appear to respond to midlife in terms of happiness or relational compatibility. In this often-tumultuous time, we might all benefit from the advice given by poet Rainer Maria Rilke to a young man who sought him out:

> Be patient toward all that is unsolved…and try to love the *questions themselves*.…Do not now seek the answers, which cannot be given you because you would not be able to live them.…*Live* the questions now. Perhaps you will then gradually…live along some distant day into the answer. (35)

Patience is the crucial virtue at this time; somehow, we must learn to bear the necessary suffering of waiting for the process to unfold. Embracing the questions themselves without necessarily finding solace in quick, facile answers is the task of maturity.

Midlife, whether we like it or not, is a time to confront life's big questions, to change our consciousness, and to open ourselves up to the larger vistas of life and the cosmos. It is a time of uncertainties—a time to wander in the wilderness of the soul, discovering new vistas of self, relationships, and faith. It is a time of destruction and recreation, of endings and new beginnings. Often that which served us well in the first half of life becomes the enemy in the second half. For example, the well-ordered, disciplined life of a military officer, accountant, or college professor may be in desperate need of spontaneity or regular intervals of silliness and play. C. G. Jung famously stated:

> The worst of it all is that intelligent and cultivated people live their lives without even knowing of the possibility of such transformations. Thoroughly unprepared we take the step into the afternoon of life; worse still, we take this step with the false assumption that our truths and ideals will serve us

as hitherto. But we cannot live the afternoon of life according to the program of life's morning; for what was great in the morning will be little at evening, and what in the morning was true will at the evening have become a lie. (*CW*, 11: 396)

Midlife offers the opportunity for change and reappraisal of our values and ideals. Often, during the first half of life, we are living up to parental values and ideals, or at least to their perspective on life. By midlife, however, the authentic self or center of our being is yearning to be heard and expressed.

I remember one forty-five-year-old woman who was confronted with the need to change a dysfunctional relationship in her life. With the support of friends, Elizabeth began to look honestly at this relationship and the ways in which it had affected her, both positive and negative. Meeting with a therapist, she began to realize that the relationship was more complicated than she had at first thought. It was enmeshed with her own parental issues and unfinished business with other men in her life. As Elizabeth began to face the daunting task of unpacking the baggage of this relationship, she wondered how she might best focus her work. Her therapist recommended that she consider a "letting-go" ritual. At first, Elizabeth felt overwhelmed at the prospect, and quite unqualified to do such a thing, but after composing herself, she began by thinking of what she wanted to *say* through the ritual. Slowly, over a period of several days, different ideas coalesced into a meaningful whole. She chose a couple of multivocal symbols to express her conflicted feelings, along with a dramatic action, and then decided what she needed to speak out loud. After choosing a sacred place to enact the ritual, she asked one of her friends to witness the ritual with her. This ritual expression was not only enlightening but liberating for Elizabeth; she experienced a newfound depth and inner power of renewal in herself, and this experience continues to nourish and sustain her as she proceeds through midlife, facing other issues with newfound confidence. Elizabeth learned that her interior life is created for wholeness and individuation, and that as she cooperates with this soulful expression of union, she will indeed discover greater happiness.

A ritual, when done effectively, can guide the participants back to the original wound where the unfinished business can be completed. At midlife, this is especially applicable. Ironically, it is this wound, so often consciously avoided, that can be the doorway to the sacred, the divine, and the desired healing.

Cultural anthropologist Ronald Grimes warns that we must face such emotionally charged life events directly and consciously, or worse may happen:

> The primary work of a rite of passage is to ensure that we attend to such events fully, which is to say, spiritually, psychologically, and socially. Unattended, a major life passage can become a yawning abyss, draining off psychic energy, engendering social confusion, and twisting the course of the life that follows it. Unattended passages become spiritual sinkholes around which hungry ghosts, those greedy personifications of unfinished business, hover. (*Deeply into the Bone*, 5–6)

In my experience, Rilke's advice to "love the questions themselves" is often more easily adopted by women, who commonly find themselves at midlife with a series of questions that are less about achievement and more about relationship and "my place in the world." Events like the departure of the children from the parental home (the so-called empty nest syndrome); the retirement of the woman herself from her career; or even more challenging, some women would say, the retirement of the husband from his; the need for the discovery of herself as a person, rather than as a mother, wife, caregiver, and on on; the desire to find her own voice, as her outside interests expand; and, not least, the issue of responsibility for the care of aging parents.

How will a woman successfully embrace these major life passages where the potential exists for her to be pulled in many different directions? Typically, she will be aware of the changes to come, through her network of relationships, and will share her fears and anxieties with other women. This situation leads more easily into the area where ritual might be utilized: an established "witnessing community" may well be at hand; sharing and preparation may already be taking place, so that a ritual marking some of these life developments might be more readily accessible. I know of a group of women who took that virtually universal feminine experience of menopause and decided to honor it with a ritual. For them, it was a positive way of respecting three realities: their embodiment, their aging, and their maturing womanhood.

The ritual arose out of their own discussions and sharing—often in a humorous vein—the *trials and tribulations* of the physical aspects of menopause, but also the changes that were taking place in their lives alongside the biological transition. Present also was the notion of them being welcomed into the status of elder. This is how they did it:

- They asked a group of postmenopausal women friends to form the witnessing community; one of these women acted as facilitator.
- They chose a suitable piece of literature to read aloud.
- Each woman spoke briefly of the things she wanted to leave behind: thoughts and beliefs

and fears she no longer needed, and of the hopes and the fears she had for the future, as her body aged and her horizons changed.

At the conclusion of each woman's spoken words, one from the witnessing community presented her with a bouquet of flowers, accompanied by words of affirmation and encouragement. Here was the multivocal symbol (Turner), accompanied by performative words (Rappaport). The flowers functioned as a symbol of the full flowering of the woman's beauty, her maturity, the diversity of her own gifts, and the color with which she lit up the world around her. This symbol also spoke to these women of their fragility, their mortality, and the transient nature of life itself; simultaneously, there was reference to the potentiality of each woman's life blooming where it was planted.

Here the symbol incorporates the conflicting elements present in an aging woman: the feeling of conventional beauty versus the beauty of maturity, wisdom, and age; no longer life bearing in the physical sense versus a generative life of grandmother or elder. Perhaps one reason that our society has not developed a ritual to honor menopause is that we have such conflicted feelings about the aging process in women. But here we have all the elements of good ritual. It was a powerfully affirming, transforming experience for all the women involved.

For a man, the midlife transition process appears to be more task-oriented. Psychologists Daniel Levinson and Murray Stein have proposed the following set of tasks as a means for a man to achieve this transition in a healthy manner:

- Confronting one's limitations
- Befriending one's interior life
- Realignment of one's central focus
- Discerning one's life task or work of service

If a man is to complete these tasks, he may need to nurture certain qualities previously, perhaps, underutilized.

Confronting one's limitations: These limitations include mortality, the ongoing aging process, the death of childhood or adolescent dreams, the ending of an era in my life. I must accept the unpalatable truth: I am no longer young. The quality needed for this task is humility.

Befriending one's interior life: The challenge is to learn about and embrace our interior landscape, which includes the unlived parts of life, as well as our feminine or creative side. This means discovering ways of integrating oppositional tendencies or polarities in our soul. The man must discover meaning or deeper joy in his life. The quality needed for this task is openness.

Realignment of one's central focus: Rather than seeking to meet the expectations of others, the man relates to life's demands from the authentic self. Discernment is needed so that what is not real or important can be discarded. The quality needed for this task is fortitude or courage for the long haul.

Discerning of one's life task or work of service: The exploration of the reasons for my existence might pose the question: "To what cause/person/group might I offer service in the second half of my life?" The answer may prompt a change of career or a commitment to a neighborhood or global project. The quality needed for this task is creative imagination.

Rituals assist us in connecting with the inner polarities of the soul. As Levinson pointed out in his research, this is the work of midlife—integrating opposing tendencies within our life. Translating this into action is another challenge. Dramatic action moves people much more readily into a new way of being or thinking, and therefore into a new way of acting. This ritual action startles the mind into awareness through the senses. From the soul's perspective, ritual and reality are two sides of the same coin. Therefore, to live the symbolic life is to live authentically with a religious framework.

For individuation to take place, we must practice the art of integration, rather than the all-too-common practice of scapegoating as a means of feeling superior to others. Projections, attractions, and repulsions can aid the psyche in identifying and reclaiming the "lost gold" from our shadow, especially in midlife. The highly charged impulses, drives, fantasies, longings, and wishes of adolescence make a powerful reappearance, but often in unexpected and unplanned ways (such as promiscuity, addiction, compulsive activity, or materialism). This unconscious eruption brings to the fore the rejected parts of the personality previously left unattended or underdeveloped in the first half of life. The seeds of individuation dwell in the neglected figures that now persistently call for restoration and attention (Stein, 74–78). What is missing in the conscious world can be discovered in the unconscious.

This is what ritual does for us. It connects desire and action, so that there is an effective change. This change invariably affects the body politic, for the ritual is not ego-centered as much as it is centered on transformation. Other means of expression that have been put forth as ritual for some participants include sandplay therapy, psychodrama, and theater as ritual. The proof of its validity, as authentic ritual, however, is in the transformative element.

The breaking open or bridging of ego-consciousness with the unconscious is essential for authentic transformation or individuation to occur. But how do we build this bridge? By recognizing that opposites temper and restore each other, we can discover the inner courage and humility to interact with the shadow. The addition of the neglected elements brings wholeness. The light and the darkness combine for a dynamic balance or tolerance of ambiguity and paradox. This is the mark of adult maturity—to hold the interior oppositions in tension without becoming overwhelmed by them. Or as psychoanalyst Robert Johnson says: "No redemption of one in a pair of opposites is possible without the same redemption for the other" (*Transformation*, 95).

Without the avenue of ritualized liberation, the possibility of a person being torn asunder by his or her interior demons, or of wreaking havoc on society, increases dramatically. However, the realm of imagination, symbol, and ritual can offer helpful solutions to this dilemma. We can face the midlife problems of meaninglessness, loneliness, and the reclamation of the unlived parts of life consciously—and much more wisely—by incorporating imaginal symbols into meaningful rituals. These symbols can be created from some of the most mundane, everyday objects, such as a dead branch, a hole in the ground, a large boulder, ashes, an old college sweater, a trophy, water, fire, or an empty bottle. The list is endless.

Nature teaches us that the ability to survive and flourish depends upon the flexibility and adaptability of the organism. It is the same for us. The psychological purpose of midlife transition is to bring about a fuller sense of self-awareness or consciousness. It is about a growing flexibility and adaptability in the face of the ongoing aging process. It is in this transitional space or liminality that we have the opportunity to realize: "I am a Self and not only a function, an ego" (Stein, 60–61). This is why so many of us question our careers at midlife: "Who am I, apart from my career, my responsibilities?" "How is it that I feel stuck, or that I am going in reverse?" "Why do I feel out of control?" "Is this all there is?"

What, then, is the key to midlife recovery for a man? I believe it is this: He needs to know his parameters or limitations in order to "play the game" or execute the task. Once he grasps this information, he is ready for the goal or task to be accomplished. Everything changes in the second half of life—the rules of engagement, the goals, and the methodology. No wonder it's difficult for a man to maneuver in this strange terrain. He feels like a stranger in his own life.

My own experience, both personal and professional, is that men need some kind of help to make the midlife crossing. We cannot do this alone. I have observed that men turn to fathers, brothers, uncles, mentors, psychotherapists, co-workers, and friends, seeking assistance for the necessary shifts that have to be made. A rite of passage that focuses on the tasks of midlife, as outlined previously, can appropriately assist in this process.

When a midlife crisis forces them into a dialogue with their soul, men are ripe for a spiritual encounter. Again, from my own experience, it seems that the context and a disciplined attentiveness to the task are everything. The rites of passage might be a three- to seven-day process, a series of weekend retreats, or a series of planned weekly meetings, punctuated by a couple of professionally guided retreats. The requirements of effective masculine ritual are straightforward. The experience must be clear and direct and contextualized within a particular time and space. It ought ideally to take place in nature, where the rugged interior of a man confronts the cosmos on its own terms. The ritual needs to be challenging, perhaps almost brutal, in a way, in order to push the man to his limits, to assist him in breaking through to something new. Finally, the ritual must be simple and uncomplicated, with few words and symbols. It need not be ponderous or belabored (Groves).

It is this experience or state of liminality that Rev. Richard Rohr, OFM, seeks to create for men in midlife transition as they enter his experiential program Men's Rite of

Passage (MROP). Where adolescent rites of initiation follow the hero archetype, Rohr seeks to tap into the magician and king archetypal structures. Archetypes are to the soul what the senses are to the body. They are a way of "reading" reality through symbols. The MROP consists of a five-day wilderness retreat experience incorporating Jewish and Christian mythologies and symbols. Rohr builds on the work of Eliade, van Gennep, and Turner, following a dynamic three-part pattern of rites of passage. Reframing this patterned work of van Gennep through the lens of Christian mythology, it would look like this: The first stage of separation is the path of suffering, or *via purgativa*, wherein we confront death in all its many forms. The second stage of transition is the path of grace, or *via illuminativa*. This is the stage of actual initiation when our consciousness is transformed. The final stage of return is the path of communion, or *via unitiva*, wherein we are received back into community as a new or resurrected man.

Rohr uses the vehicle of metaphorical language to stir the cauldron of the men's souls. Taking the role of the wise elder, he weaves together images, metaphors, analogies, and symbols from these two traditional religious mythologies to create an ambiance that is conducive to transformation. Rohr is able to open a doorway to the men's souls in a manner that permits everything and everyone to feel welcomed. As a result, questions about meaning, life, self, relationships, and the Divine come pouring forth. These questions are distilled and processed in a setting that incorporates times of solitude and silence, balanced with small, in-home discussion groups. Ritual drumming helps the men to make the move from their heads and intellectual ruminations into the world of the soul. The focal point of these days though is the procession of transformative rituals that serve as carriers and containers for the men's work.

Having experienced and facilitated the MROP, I have witnessed firsthand the efficacy of this ritual. I have talked to a number of men across the spectrum of life experiences who have participated in these rites of passage and they have confirmed my own experience and perception. The MROP has been presented more than forty times throughout the world, with similar success. "The point of initiations, whether accidental or intentional, is to touch the mysterious core, pass through change, and return....One touch can change the course of a life forever" (Meade, *Men and the Water*, 431). This MROP experience becomes, in effect, a second birth of the spirit.

How does it work? It works for all the reasons outlined above and reiterated below. There is an archetypal predisposition of people for initiation, which yearns for meaning and the integration of one's life. The screening for these rites assists the men to discern if they are truly ready for this experience at this time in their life. Careful preparation and attention to the details of the rites set the stage for this creative dynamic. Trained elders guide the process of the active embodied participation of each individual. There is also an active interaction between the polarities of the men's psyche as each man wrestles with his own inner *demons* within the sacred space. The personal and communal shadow is consciously engaged throughout the entire process, making it authentic. The participants have a respect for liminality and altered states of reality, which opens them up to an experience of the invisible reality through the ritual process. These transforming rituals engage both the body and the psyche. The symbols used are multivocal and deeply meaningful to the participants. There is, most important, a dynamic balance between silence and words spoken. Words are used sparingly, to "keep the edges hot" and the focus on the interior reality of transformation. There is also plenty of time for personal reflection and the sharing of the men's individual experience of the rites. The presence of the male witnessing community strengthens and sustains the effects of this communal experience for each man. Follow-up continues to sustain and support this important work.

This "embodied way of knowing" (Grillo) in a sacred space is a new experience for many of these men and so impacts them with a greater force, giving them a new cosmology, a different way of belonging and connecting to the universe. This is the real work of religion—to help people to see and experience reality as it is, not as they would like it to be. Jung is purported to have commented that the field of depth psychology emerged only because religion had moved away from engaging the fullness of the depths of the human psyche. For this reason, it is imperative that this work between the two realms is mediated through symbols. As the late Trappist monk Thomas Merton pointed out: "the true symbol does not merely point to something else. It contains in itself a structure which awakens our consciousness to the inner meaning of life and of reality itself. A true symbol takes us to the center of the circle, not to another point on the circumference" (340). In other words, directly experiencing the symbol transforms the individual.

Creating rituals for midlife transition is a vital part of supporting and vitalizing the human developmental process. It assists in the work of moving the individual along the road of maturity. Is it possible then that one can do this ritual work alone without the witnessing presence of the community? Certainly, it is possible, but the presence of the witnesses serves to hold the participant accountable to the change and to his or her commitments.

Kathleen Wall and Gary Ferguson, in their book, *Rites of Passage: Celebrating Life's Changes*, relate the story of a ritual created by a man named David as a means of orienting himself to the polarities of midlife. No outward stresses or crises precipitated this decision to do the ritual. He simply wanted to make the midlife shift more real, more meaningful. David realized that this was just the first step in a long process of midlife changes.

David used the mountain cabin of a friend as the sacred space to participate in his weekend ritual. After arriving on Friday night, he cooked dinner and had a good night's sleep. The next morning, he arose before dawn and took a long hot bath, after which he dressed in the oldest, most tattered clothing he owned. He took his backpack and headed out to the woods where he found a sacred spot from which to view the sunrise. Then he began a ceremony of forgiveness for all those with whom he had unfinished business: a high-school teacher, his father, who died early in his life, and his eldest daughter. Next, he participated in a ritual of openness by digging a hole in the ground as a symbol of his openness to whatever was to come next into his life. He placed kernels of corn in the hole, naming the values that he wanted to high-light in the second half of his life. Afterward, he buried the kernels and placed a flower on top of the mound.

Later that day, David honored the polarities in his life by placing four stones in a circle. He took a substantial amount of time to sit with each stone (polarity) and reflect upon how he could embrace the paradox of both extremes of these polarities. He committed himself to a particular active response to be completed the following week.

As a final ritual act, David removed his old clothes, and burned them in the cabin's wood stove. He then ceremoni-ally donned a new set of clothes, signifying his shift in per-sonhood (Wall and Ferguson, 148–52). David reflected on his experience thus:

Since that ritual, I have been seeing things with different eyes. Part of it has been my work at the youth center; in those surroundings I notice things I wouldn't have otherwise. The work keeps me connected to what I value. But there's more to it. The world is different everywhere. It's as if by declaring in ritual what I wanted to create, I started seeing the raw materials lying all around me. (Wall and Ferguson, 153)

Since that weekend experience, David has returned periodically to the site of his ritual for reflection and reconnection. He has also become more aware of the many opportunities to mark life events with ritual and ceremony. This is a wonderful example of how ritual assists the individual to move forward in life with less emotional encumbrances and more happiness.

Questions for Personal Reflection:

- What nagging questions, doubts, yearnings need to be ritually acknowledged in my life?
- What relationships (past or present) are *out of order* and need to be reconciled?
- What do I need to let go of in order to move forward in my life? How might I ritualize that letting go?

Questions for Parish Leaders:

- How might we facilitate movement for those *emotionally stuck* in a particular relationship or situation?

- What do we offer adults in midlife situations?
- Is there an opportunity for men and women to dialogue among and between themselves about these issues?

Tips for Parish Leaders:

- Connect men and women with retreat experiences that speak to this topic.
- Create rituals that can be used for specific situations in midlife (e.g., divorce, forced or voluntary retirement, long-term illness, or failure).
- Be attentive to the "sandwich generation" as they care for children and elderly parents. Are their needs, hopes, and anxieties being pastorally attended to in an effective way? Is there a place for ritual here?

5

Relationships: The Dangerous Minefield

NOWHERE IS THE GAP in our ritual repertoire more apparent than in the area of our relationships and the way they are initiated, expressed, nurtured, reconciled, or even terminated. The existence of such a gap is most clearly seen within the family structures of our society. With no ritual framework to regularly assist the work of intimacy within families, we are left with words, and silence—often misinterpreted. The real issues are frequently never completely addressed. Misunderstandings are multiplied, and needless separations can be created. Rituals are too potent a tool of expression to be left solely within the sanctuary.

Therapist David Feinstein observes:

[C]ontemporary society is typified by a poverty of vibrant rituals—ceremonies that are connected to the deeper realms of human existence, the realms traditionally touched by mythology. This bankruptcy of meaningful ritual in American homes is seen by some anthropologists as representing cultural decay. One of the first things to occur when a primitive culture begins to deteriorate under the impact of the West is that the ceremonial systems disintegrate. This leads to internal disorganization, loss of values and social fragmentation. At the very least, our lack of ritual signals a period of massive transition in our cultural beliefs and practices. (Feinstein and Mayo, 42)

Generally speaking, the fundamental setting for human life, at least at some point, is the family. For this reason, it is appropriate to turn our attention to the various opportunities in family life that present themselves for ritual enactment. Family life, in all its various expressions, can engender strong emotions, positive and negative. It is here, in the crucible of family relatedness, that people generally are socialized to the important themes of communal relationship and intimacy. Ritual can help the family unit as a whole, and individual members in particular, to negotiate the challenges of intense emotional intercourse. Well-planned rituals can focus the participants on the issue that needs to be addressed, and engage them in a manner that can be liberating and unifying at the same time. Good ritual is paradoxical in nature in that it interacts with both sides of an issue. Through the careful use of a few meaningful symbols and well-chosen words, the participants are enabled to express the inexpressible in a liberating manner, which may well be nonverbal.

Facing our fears of intimacy is always very difficult, even for the most mature among us. However, we are created for intimacy and must necessarily face these fears directly, or we will tend to fill the void with unhealthy choices that lead to a desiccated life. We end up settling for superficial relationships and conversations, never tasting the depth of what it means to be truly human—in relationship. We then treat our possessions as persons (even naming them!) and persons as objects (witness the rise in online pornography as well as the emotional pornography that fills the newsstands). In our culture, use of the Internet, text messaging, Facebook, and e-mail has dramatically risen, leaving us with the question:

Does this really satisfy our need for intimacy? Are we escaping the intimacy we really crave? Rather than face-to-face intimacy, with voice and eye contact, are we escaping into a world of make-believe and distance? Rituals assist and power us into greater intimacy. Often we find ourselves saying and doing things in ritual space that are so direct and truthful that we are left in a state of unitive contentment.

A number of opportunities in family life present themselves for ritual expression. Each of these possibilities is a doorway into greater intimacy and mutual understanding. Life-cycle and lifestyle changes, especially within and between family structures or generations, are enormously complicated and can be fraught with conflicted emotions. This is where ritual can assist as part of the process in developing or deepening family intimacy. As a former youth minister, I discovered this truth repeatedly in my dealings with family dynamics.

Like many men, I have struggled with intimacy issues with my father: needing to understand him, to accept him as he is, and to be interiorly at peace with him, even though our ideologies often conflicted. Several years ago, as a means toward healing and strengthening our relationship, I invited my father on an intensive five-day men's retreat. In between the conferences, we would sequester ourselves to discuss a range of issues. I sensed that my father was feeling threatened by my probing questions, so I changed my tactic. I asked him to tell the story of his life and of his relationship with his parents and grandparents. As he began to relate his story, I comprehended his pain more compassionately. I understood why I had not received what I really wanted from him—nor he from me. At the conclusion of his story, I realized that it was time for me to let go of my resentment toward him so that each of us could begin to deepen and appreciate our relationship. I then asked him if he would be willing to participate, with me, in a ritual that would express the liberation we both sought. He agreed. After some discussion and reflection, we planned the ritual together and a week later we went to the banks of a nearby river, where we enacted that liberation to which we had committed ourselves. In that liminal space in the wilderness, I told my father that I wanted to let go of all the judgments, hurts, and resentments against him. He asked my forgiveness, and I gave it to him, imagining all that dark, negative stuff being thrown into the river. I, in turn, asked his forgiveness for the times that I, as his son, had hurt him or not lived up to his hopes or expectations or kept him at a distance. My father then gave me a large portrait of himself in his military uniform from World War II, with the words: "This is for you. This is the only time in my life I felt like a hero." His symbolic gift deeply touched me. I then gave him a drumstick with the teasing words: "This is for you. It's time for you to go and beat on your own drum now and not mine." This was in reference to his habit of introducing himself as the father of a priest, rather than acknowledging his own considerable worth. He smiled, and then we hugged each other, leaving that sacred place with our hearts full. This simple and profound ritual was transformative for us. Our relationship changed considerably since that day. Now that my father has passed away, I more clearly recognize the significance of that liberating ritual. It freed me to bid him farewell with grace and understanding, rather than regrets for what might have been.

Anthropologists have observed that ritual has several functions that enhance the dynamics of social cohesion and individual happiness:

- the enrichment of community
- the ordering and transforming of our lives

- the bridging of ego consciousness and the unconscious that can lead to an experience of the Divine
- the facilitation of developmental change and transition

Ritualist Ronald Grimes insists that rituals must not be simply inherited and repeated without reflection and contextualization. This means that there are different modes of ritual, to be used according to the context of the community and the needs of the participants. Rituals are always in the process of being re-created, as each generation interweaves its own tales with those of its ancestors. The ever-changing human narrative calls for a ritual newness that is birthed in its encounter with the Divine narrative.

One challenging situation in family life is the emotional confusion that a child who moves constantly between his or her biological parents can experience. The introduction of some healthy ritualizing behaviors might ease this: The parent and child could regularly enjoy a meal at a favorite restaurant, watch a movie, or walk through the park together. In this way, the child is offered a sense of grounding and a way of reconnecting. Ritualizing behaviors, while not offering transformation, can provide opportunities for comfort, order, and connection. Such behaviors would not necessarily negate the need for ritual but could serve as a preparation process or foundation, leading to a specific ritual. In the situation being described here, should there be a dramatic change or development in the child's situation (e.g., one of the parents moves to another city or remarries), the child might then be open to a specific ritual that would embody and express the new challenge and help him or her move into it with confidence.

Another situation in which ritualizing behavior might enhance family intimacy is in the area of communication.

There are some families who organize regular family gatherings in a special place where a "talking stick" is passed from one person to the other as each has something to say, while the other family members listen attentively. This practice could provide a heightened sense of focus and mutual respect as the conversation unfolds. Consciously observing various daily ritualizing behaviors together as a family (e.g., eating meals, playing, or working together) can also create a more cohesive sense of belonging and connection.

Family rituals help to ease the tension of transition and to express the inexpressible as individuals, or the family as a whole, move forward. Such times might include the following: moving households, a child starting school, transitioning from childhood to preadolescence, or leaving one school for another. The loss of a pet, recovery from a major failure, death anniversaries, a change in discipline, or a child entering adolescence are other situations that come to mind. I know of one family that planned and prepared a lovely ritual to mark leaving their home of twenty years. They each lit a candle and went from room to room, sharing memories of events in each. Tears and laughter filled these empty rooms as they recalled their family narrative. Then they each in turn extinguished the candle, with a prayer for the new owners.

At first glance, these experiences might appear to be minor occurrences in a "normal" family environment that need no acknowledgment, but they are the meaningful strands of a personal, familial, and social narrative that will continue to play out over time. This is about building and protecting the web of a family's memories in a respectful manner.

Family rituals accompanying graduation ceremonies can be most empowering for the individual and family community. Joining the public and private aspects of these stages of academic development through ritual expression often strengthens communal relationships. The same principle applies with engagement parties, baby showers, naming ceremonies, and birthday celebrations, when consciously and thoughtfully planned. This is about honoring the need for social coherence and tradition within a new complex reality. I believe that ritual can bridge this paradoxical tension, if it is used appropriately.

Ritual works best when the facilitators or participants make use of symbols and dramatic action that are grounded in the culture and experience of the participants. The power of ritual is heightened by the deliberate creation of space around the provocative experience. This is what is often missing in our dominant culture—the space of silence and solitude around the significant experiences of life. One great love or death experience is enough to ready us for transformation if we are willing to pay attention and absorb the lesson. However, without taking the time to authentically integrate the lesson, and enter it fully, we are left to bury, deny, project, or flee from it. The result: no transformation and the transmission of my own pain onto others. For example, a person who has experienced rejection or abandonment from one or both parents might continue to live out this emotional trauma in clinging, needy relationships with friends and acquaintances.

Adult children coming back home temporarily or permanently, for whatever reason, might benefit by expressing ritually any conflicted feelings they have about the return. They now relate differently within the family structures. It could be as simple as the investment of time collaborating on a written covenant that spells out mutual responsibilities and expectations, followed by a celebratory glass of wine or a meal. Relationships are perhaps the single greatest cause of both happiness and heartache in the life of a human being. One of the first steps in coming to maturity in relationships with others is the acquisition of self-knowledge and self-acceptance. From this standpoint, we are then capable of a freely chosen interdependent relationship in which the best in us calls to the best in others, helping them to grow along with us.

Ritual can be of tremendous value to those of us seeking to improve our relationships. The following is a story of one man's successful use of ritual in the midst of just such a situation. Michael is a colleague of mine, a man in midlife, who was struggling in his relationship with his mother. It had devolved into a codependent, enmeshed relationship. He had become almost a surrogate spouse, in emotional terms, for his mother and felt caught in her multiple needs. Michael recognized that a change was needed for the good of the relationship. There was a need and a desire to move into a healthy adult relationship of mutuality and interdependence. He approached his mother to discuss his feelings, thoughts, and desire to improve the relationship. She agreed that change was needed. He proposed the idea of creating a ritual as a way of achieving what they both recognized was necessary. After much thought, discussion, and reflection, they decided upon a neutral site for the ritual. By fortunate accident, the opportunity presented itself to perform the ritual in a foreign country. Their first symbolic action was to draw a circle, creating a space that they mutually acknowledged as "sacred." They then spoke briefly of attachments they needed to jettison, and of the ways in which they wanted to reshape their relationship. To symbolize this shift, they offered each other small gifts, embraced each other, and then stepped outside the circle into their new reality. This ritual changed Michael's life. He felt liberated from the need to meet every emotional demand he perceived in his mother. He felt like a new man. In conversations with me, he has described the changes in his mother's attitudes and behavior, which appear to indicate that her life, too, was changed by this ritual.

This story illustrates the manner in which ritual can effectively contain the polarities of a relationship through an embodied, symbolic expression. In that liminal space, Michael and his mother were able to hold together the past, the present reality, and their desire for the future of the relationship. The symbolic action of exchange of the physical gifts, the words, and the embrace powered them forward into a mutually respectful and interdependent, rather than a dependent, relationship. Thus by attending to planning, to the shadow side of themselves, to geographical location, brevity of speech, and meaningful symbolic action, these two people experienced the transformative power of ritual.

The use of rituals or psychodrama in the process of therapy can help the family to reacquire affective ritualized behavior. "Rituals provide models, sanction transitions, and aid in the expression of emotions. Some rituals give family members the possibility of exploring themselves deeply, providing meaning to their lives, and giving them a feeling of belonging and sense of commitment. They allow individual freedom, while preserving intimacy and bonds" (Imber-Black, 381). We might recognize this in the story of the outcast leper who received the healing touch and compassionate welcome of Jesus (Mark 1:40–47). First are the performative words: "I do choose. Be made clean"; then the ritual action and symbolic gesture of touch, which had been denied him in his illness; finally, he is sent back into community. The man was given a new way of receiving in order that he might share with others. This he did, with real enthusiasm (1:46). This was the final sign of his complete transformation.

Friendships are another arena where ritual expression can help us to manage and negotiate the wide variety of relationships we enjoy outside the family circle. I am thinking here of work acquaintances, school friends, neighbors, long-term partnerships, community relationships, and even our intimate friends. Is there a place for a simple ritual celebration of friendships in our contemporary society? In our high-tech, low-touch culture, we can begin to face our fears of intimacy and express them in creative ways. Sociologists tell us that far more people are dying from lack of love than lack of sex, but our culture is sadly deficient in love education. Read the biblical story of David and Jonathan to see how the bond of friendship was ritually honored by these two men (1 Sam 18:1–5).

I now turn to a more intimate form of relationship— marriage. Anthropologist Arnold van Gennep, in surveying wedding rites across cultures, discovered three central themes in the ceremonies:

- rites of separation from the family of origin
- rites of union for the couple
- rites of incorporation into the new extended family

He describes these marriage processes in the cultures he studied as taking place gradually over time, with the various segments performed sequentially. Van Gennep's insights might assist us in our contemporary challenge of making wedding ceremonies more meaningful and transformative.

Wedding ceremonies can be made more meaningful in several ways. Often couples choose a traditional ceremony without much thought of personalizing it or researching what they really want to express. Their focus is often diminished by the myriad details surrounding this momentous occasion. In order to create a memorable wedding experience, it is necessary to prepare with great care and thought for this momentous life transition and to individually honor the different themes of the ceremony. In this way, the ceremony can become a transformative ritual rather than a pleasant exchange to be performed in anticipation of the wedding reception.

Weaving together narrative and ritual over a period of time brings power and depth to the wedding ceremony and might do the same for the relationship. Family narratives need to be heard so that family myths can be honored by both partners. This can best be done in premarital counseling, for example, often through the use of a genogram, or the exploration of family symbols. Because weddings involve the joining of two families, the theme of "leaving" one's family or parents needs to be addressed, along with "cleaving" to the new spouse. This is extremely helpful for a smooth transition.

Our ancestors knew how to honor both departure movements: The two stages were ritualized separately, and, thus, clear markers were provided for the transition that was occurring. Until the Middle Ages, the private promise of love became a public reality in the ritual of betrothal. This rite of separation initiated the time of engagement. It was a public acknowledgment of departure from one's home of origin that included a parental blessing (Stevenson, 57). The modern wedding ceremony, combining the two stages of betrothal and marital incorporation, can be overloaded with too much emotional weight. While some religious traditions do offer blessing rituals for the newly engaged, these rituals are often ignored or underused. The wedding then can become a single mythic event that stands alone, isolated, and unrelated to anything that precedes or follows it.

How might we gather in and honor the human history being brought into the union of the man and woman in marriage so that authenticity and mutuality might be strengthened and deepened? As a ritual elder, I have sometimes given the couple a questionnaire for their parents to complete prior to the wedding, as part of the process of welcoming their new son- or daughter-in-law into the family. The parents were asked about their own marriage preparation, their own wedding ceremony, and their expectations for the about-to-be married couple. Then, at the beginning of the marriage ceremony, the parents were publicly recognized and affirmed for their role in bringing their son or daughter to this day and were asked to affirm their support for the marriage. This can also work very effectively with stepparents.

Marriage is a place where projections of all kinds often run rampant. How can we address this shadow aspect in the wedding service? A person does a grave disservice to his or her partner by projecting his or her image of goodness—or of darkness—onto the other. Psychoanalyst Robert Johnson relates the story of an about-to-be married couple who showed great creativity in confronting this issue:

> The night before their marriage they held a ritual where they made their "shadow vows." The groom said, "I will give you an identity and make the world see you as an extension of myself." The bride replied, "I will be compliant and sweet, but underneath I will have the real control. If anything goes wrong, I will take your money and your house." They then drank champagne and laughed heartily at their foibles, knowing that in the course of the marriage, these shadow figures would inevitably come out. (*Owning Your Own Shadow*, 64–65)

These shadow figures will continue to emerge during the course of their marriage, since they are a key component of the human psyche. No one can eliminate the presence or effects of the shadow. All we can do is become aware of its various components and learn how to engage them with respect. By beginning their married life with a shadow ritual, this couple was publicly honoring an important part of their relationship and will be much more aware of the inner workings of the shadow and how to manage it in healthy ways.

Ritual has a way of expressing eternal and cultural truths that reach beyond and within human situations. Rituals practiced with no concern for the context or the time become empty and meaningless. What worked well in the past may not work psychologically in the present, and vice versa. Such dead rituals then descend into mere ceremony with no capacity for transformation. Good ritual must express some aspect of the shadow; otherwise, it is ceremony, marking an event.

What, then, makes a wedding a ceremony rather than a ritual? Typically, weddings are ceremonies; they function as an acknowledgment of the status quo, with a great many words, numerous symbols, no acknowledgment of the shadow, and usually no transformation element for anyone. Transformation for the couple, however, can take place when:

- The performative words ("I, Ben, commit myself to you, Linda") are both privately and publicly owned. This will have been achieved through extensive reflection and discussion with a significant investment of time.
- The symbolic element is limited, focused, and personally meaningful, rather than extravagant, showy, and culturally conformist.
- There is authentic engagement with the shadow of their relationship.
- Liminal space has been created.

Thus, ritual is created, and transformation is possible for the couple.

The wedding itself—the wording of the vows, the movements, the particular symbols—ought to express the deepest values of the couple. In order for ritual to be grounded in reality, it is essential that the polarities in the relationship are addressed and the shadow is honored—thus, in good times and in bad, in sickness and in health. If the couple or the family members involved are more focused on the show rather than the substance, it might be that underlying relationship issues or family skeletons are being masked. Rituals can sometimes unlock opportunities for healing and reconciliation within the family structure.

Because the wedding is such a key component of an ongoing process of community building and strengthening of family relationships, the work of ritual here is important. In the words of anthropologist Roy Rappaport, "there is a special relationship between ritual and performativeness" (115). This is particularly apparent in weddings (e.g., "I now pronounce you man and wife"). Therefore, the words to the couple and between the couple are to be chosen with great care. It is these "performative utterances" that are so essential to the efficacy of the ritual (Rappaport). Too many words or ill-chosen words can spoil the effect.

Remarriages present a different challenge: that of incorporating into the wedding ceremony the fuller family narratives, as well as an acknowledgment of any children from previous marriages. Such a process might make possible a more comfortable future for all concerned. What might this look like in ritual space?

Dealing with conflict is a painful but necessary part of all relationships. Simple rituals of healing and reconciliation can help a couple or family to move through such difficult situations with greater ease. It will almost always involve both parties being heard by the other at a level deeper than that of the presenting issue. Once the process of listening and rapprochement has been attended to, the parties need to perform a ritual action to cement the reconciliation. This is another example of ritual functioning as a vehicle for the ongoing maintenance of the family structure.

Therapist Onno Van der Hart relates an intriguing story of a couple who used ritual as an important adjunct to counseling, to establish a new level of commitment in their marriage, after infidelity on the part of the husband. With the help of a counselor, the couple decided to mark their transition with a ritual. They each selected one of their wedding gifts, drove down to the docks, and cast the presents into the sea. For them, this act symbolized a casting-off of the first part of their marriage and initiated a new chapter in their lives together (in Wall and Ferguson, 30). It freed them from the pain of betrayal and enabled them to absorb and integrate the benefits of the counseling. This successful ritual act facilitated a new chapter in their lives marked by a sense of hope and purpose.

A ritual of this kind offers a couple the opportunity to externalize conflicted feelings and to symbolize them in a respectful manner. A careful choice of the performative words of disengagement, spoken or written, is an essential component of the process of releasing the emotions of both parties. A commitment to disengage could also take written form, being signed by both parties and witnessed by a third party. As always in ritual, the words should be few and focused. They should reflect ownership by both parties through the process of prior discussion and reflection.

The potential harm is especially real for couples going through a divorce. Because divorce is such a common occurrence in our culture, I would like to take a long look at this phenomenon. Since our culture offers no public ritual or ceremony to mark this legal event, the experience of divorce is sometimes like an open wound that can continue to infect and harm the two people involved, as well as their community, for years to come. There is no real closure or transformation. The only symbol is the divorce decree itself. Looking at divorce proceedings symbolically, we can observe the process of a ritualized shadow form of "undating" and "disengagement," whereby the shadow material of both individuals is given voice in the public forum of the court, with court-appointed witnesses. The sacred space becomes the court rather than a church or synagogue. I believe that the process ought to be given more respect and intentionality, so that the couple might move through the grieving process more quickly with less covert violence. How different this situation could be for the couple divorcing if they were to plan a divorce ritual that, with intentionality, plumbed the depths of their pain and adequately expressed their emotions. The potential exists, of course, for hatred and aggression to prevent such a plan from being realistically acted out; the anguish of the psyche might, however, be assuaged by a ritualistic action such as tearing up a photograph, or destroying a possession of the alienated partner. It is arguable that the couple might experience healing and authentic new life much more quickly if they attended to the needs of the psyche in this way. Robert Johnson speaks of this type of exchange in the context of society:

> Ceremonies the world over, and from every age, consist mostly of destruction: sacrifice, burning, ritual killing, bloodletting, fasting, and sexual abstention. Why? These are the ritual languages that safeguard the culture by paying out the shadow in a symbolic way. It is easy to fall into the error of thinking that we protect the culture by obliterating the destructive elements. But we will see that there is no way to energize a culture except by an incorporation of them. (*Owning Your Own Shadow*, 53)

In this passage, Johnson uses the word *ceremony* in the same context in which I use the word *ritual*. While I am not advocating such bloodletting or destruction, I am saying the impulse to aggression or destruction must be given a container for symbolic expression; otherwise, it can take a literal form. When a culture or group is not willing to honor the shadow in a meaningful way, the shadow will leak out in uninvited ways, such as a terrible conflict right before the wedding ceremony, or, as has happened in my professional experience, a fit of laughter during a very proper funeral.

Sometimes, despite the best attempts of a couple, a marriage ends in divorce. This is such a painful rending of one's psyche that it necessitates a concentrated process of attentive healing. A series of personal rituals can assist this ongoing process of healing and transition into a new status in life. The estranged couple might plan an "uncoupling" ritual as a means of transitioning into the divorced state. Such a ritual would honor the mourning process that coincides with the death of a relationship. Choosing the most appropriate geographical location for this ritual is crucial for its metaphorical and social meaning.

The story of Sam provides an appropriate example. Recently divorced, he sought the help of a therapist to ritualize the painful transition in which he found himself. Sam began his ritual by standing in the middle of a circle, looking directly into the eyes of his loving family and friends gathered around him. He thanked them for their love and support. He then spoke words of disengagement from his ex-wife. His next pronouncement was one of commitment to his son, Mark, his family, and his friends. Following a moment of quiet reflection, Sam dug a hole in the ground; then he placed his wedding band in the hole. With the assistance of his father and his son, he then planted a tree over the wedding band. Those present took their turn watering the tree as a sign of their renewed commitment to relationship-building. Sam affirms that this ritual was a powerful tool in his maturing process. It signified both an ending and a beginning (Wall and Ferguson, 87–89). What makes this ritual so transformative is the conscious preparation through therapy, the engagement with the shadow, the participation of the witnessing community, the dramatic ritual action within liminal space, and the use of few words and symbols. Sam's intentionality and focus made this imaginal reality come to life in a new way.

Without such a ritual or ritual process, the psyche is often prone to act out this death experience, sometimes in chaotic ways. To enter consciously and ritually into this underworld experience takes immense courage and self-love; however, the effort is worth it. As seen from the story of Sam, it is possible to facilitate the healing process so that the person can move forward. A way is opened for the transformation of an obstacle into a stepping-stone to something new. Any person planning a divorce ritual needs to recognize and honor the broad scope of emotions involved—anger, sadness, fear, and guilt. "Ritual making at the time of divorce can be an unusual experience of antiritual. It is a moment for acknowledging thwarted dreams, for admitting ignored grace, and confessing whatever ways in which love had been withdrawn, withheld or discounted" (Anderson, 136). As in Sam's story, this is a ritual of closure, not of revenge. It reflects the desire to honor an ending in order to make way for a new beginning. Anderson continues,

> If ritual is a symbolic activity that helps individuals construct the world as a habitable place, antiritual is a sometimes necessary step for deconstructing a world that is no longer habitable and hospitable, so that another may be constructed. Antiritual is a symbolic way to pull down the empty shell of a

relationship and clear the terrain, in the hopes that
something new can be built on the same spot. (136)

While I agree with Anderson's concept, I disagree with his
use of the word *antiritual* in this situation. I believe that what
is involved is a whole new ritual of undoing or uncoupling.

Because divorce can evoke such intense emotions, the
movement forward may need to involve small steps, daily
exercises to heal the hurt. Especially, perhaps, where a marriage ritual has been deeply efficacious and the bond has
been powerful, the healing may be more difficult. Planning
a divorce ritual with one's estranged spouse carries risk
unless both parties have resolved, or attempted to resolve,
their own emotional difficulties surrounding the divorce. A
ritual of this kind offers a couple the opportunity to externalize conflicted feelings and to symbolize them in a
respectful manner. A careful choice of the performative
words of disengagement, spoken or written, is an essential
component of the process of releasing the emotions of both
parties. A commitment to disengage could also take written
form, signed by both parties and witnessed by a third.

We were created in relationship, for relationship. When
we forget this basic truth, we will tend to be unhappy and
unhealthy. Along the way, ritual helps to remind us of these
essential truths of life about right relationship and powers us
forward into change so that we can live happier lives.

Questions for Personal Reflection:

- What family relationships in my life need celebrating or reconciling?
- How can we regularly include ritual expression in our family life?
- What friendships in my life need attention?

Questions for Parish Leaders:

- Where can we assist the process of celebration and reconciliation in our parish families?
- How can we ritually honor the engagement process? Is there a way of publicly welcoming newly married couples into our faith community?
- How might we better celebrate marriages and anniversaries?

Tips for Parish Leaders:

- Ritual is a catechetical tool for expressing our faith. How might the parish staff prepare couples/ families for home celebrations?
- There is much focus on sex education in school curriculums. Could discussions with the parish school team explore a course on love educa- tion—facing issues of emotional intimacy and conflict resolution?
- What groups of people are marginalized or alienated in our parish or community (e.g., young adults, gays, elderly, youth, handicapped, particular cultures, families of prisoners, the infirm or homebound)? How might we reach out to these particular groups with rituals that honor their struggles and their aspirations?

6

Life's Losses: Love, Pain, and the Whole Damn Thing

MANY YEARS AGO, when I was a young cleric, new to parish ministry, I was approached by a young, single woman seeking my help in a difficult situation. Maria told me that she was dying from leukemia, and before she died she wanted "to walk down the main aisle of the church wearing a white dress." I was somewhat nonplussed by her request, considering her state of health. She went on to explain that all her life she had dreamed of walking down the church aisle in a white dress. Now that this was certainly not going to happen in the form of a wedding, Maria wanted to do it anyway in the form of a ceremony. I wanted to help her, and yet I knew that there existed no sacramental experience that quite fit her request. Sadly, I had to turn down her emotional request with the words: "I'm sorry but we have no sacramental expression for this type of request. If I did it for you, what about all the other single, unmarried women in the parish? What do I tell them?"

Neither Maria nor I had the language or creativity to express what she really wanted to do. I couldn't really *hear* what she was requesting because it was outside the realm of my own categories of sacramental ministry. But with the knowledge I now have, I realize that before she died she wanted to publicly honor her life with a ritual of acknowledgment and community support. Today, looking back on that encounter, I would do things very differently. I would have asked her the questions: "What is it you want to acknowledge in this ritual?" "What do you want to say to the community?" "What do you need from us?" "Are there any other symbols that hold meaning for you in this ritual expression?" "How can we create such a ritual to express this soulful desire to be recognized as someone special, important, while at the same time acknowledging your terminal illness?" I will always be grateful to Maria for stirring my awareness and sending me off into this important work of healing and reconciliation through ritual.

As the life cycle of a person unfolds, it typically opens up into new, fuller life experiences. Life changes generally involve both beginnings and endings. This often necessitates the holding and expressing of paradoxical truths such as pain and joy within a relationship, guilt and grief over a loved one's death, or conflicting beliefs about one's existence. Ritual can give impetus to the process of transformative change. It can also achieve this end by providing a safe framework for the expression of, and reflection upon, confused and self-deprecating feelings.

Kayla, a colleague of mine, illustrates this last point with her story. She recognized that she needed to ritualize a transition she was making, and she knew that for this ritual to have a transforming effect in her life, she needed to consciously immerse herself in the planning and preparation phase, making a significant investment of time. Here are her own words:

> With the planning and celebration of the ritual came strength and healing that I hadn't felt in a long time. Since then, ritual has become an important part of my life, to celebrate and mark major

changes and stages in my life. One of the rituals I prepared and celebrated was a path of my life. For months, I collected pictures and phrases, and drew images representing the major parts of my life that I wanted to let go. Using various art media, I constructed a large sheet, on which I made a path that led to a fork in the road, the point at which I began to turn my life around. At the fork, the path on the left led in the direction I did not want to take, while the path on the right led toward the goals I had set for myself, and ultimately, to heaven with God. First, I made the journey alone and then I chose three people with whom I separately walked it. As I walked the path of my life, I was able to let go of the negative events that had taken place, and that I no longer wanted to be part of who I was.

The ritual culminated in a chapel with the poster laid on the floor, ending at the altar. My mentor and I walked each step and said goodbye to that part of my life. Kneeling at the foot of the altar at the end of the path, I silently offered a prayer to God. Then I folded the path, piece by piece, and placed it on the altar, where I wrote an offering to the Lord before placing it at the foot of the cross, offering up myself to God. It was powerful to literally and figuratively let go of all the baggage I had been carrying with me for many years. Afterward, my mentor and I went to another place, where we debriefed and talked about what had just taken place.

Kayla created this ritual from her own experience with the support of her mentor. She bridged the positive and negative aspects of her life through the evocative symbol of the forked path. The debriefing afterward assisted Kayla in containing and bringing effective closure to the experience. "Ritual is more than the act itself," Kayla observed to her mentor. "It is the preparation and the debriefing afterward that make the ritual complete. With the celebration of each ritual I have done has come tremendous growth."

Kayla's story is illustrative of anthropologist Arnold van Gennep's contention that life-cycle rituals depend for their efficacy on a three-step process:

- the work of preparation
- the actual ritual event
- reincorporation into daily life

For Kayla, the debriefing aspect was the beginning step of reincorporation into her daily life. She was very clear in her own mind about the necessity and importance of all three of these steps.

At times throughout our lives, there is a need to let go not only of old, outdated roles, unhealthy relationships, emotional losses and failures, as Kayla did, but also of dreams unrealized and of unrealistic goals that are beyond our reach. Within this process, there is also a need for self-affirmation so that new beginnings can be made.

Here's a story from a men's retreat I conducted several years ago. There had been an opportunity to participate in a ritual of letting go and moving on. This ritual was based within the framework of the Native American "giving away ritual" in which an individual "gives up" or surrenders something he no longer needs, believing that someone else has need of this item. One participant was a talented young man whose dreams of playing professional baseball had proven unrealistic. His symbolic act consisted in his giving away his expensive bat to another man with the performative utterance: "This bat served me well as a baseball player when I was playing for the Philadelphia Phillies farm system; I had a lifelong dream of playing in the big leagues, but I now know that I do not have the talent for that level of play, and now it is time for me to move on." The intensity of his purpose was reflected in the mood of the group as he acknowledged this powerful transition moment. For him, the gift and the giving ceremony were a liberating experience.

It might be fair to say that, generally, ritual comes more easily to those of us who are extroverts. But what about introverts? One of my mentors related to me his own story of healing through a particular mode of ritual, which, due to the wisdom and expertise of his analyst, had been created to suit his introverted temperament. He had been experiencing recurring, distressing dreams of war and sought help in dealing with the situation. The analyst helped him to enter the dream sequence through his conscious breath. In this totally alive and embodied experience, a memory emerged into consciousness of himself as a World War II soldier in the European theater pinned down by artillery fire, unable to help a wounded comrade. The analyst then guided him through a process of reconciliation with his comrade. The client left the session feeling vibrant and transformed. Ritual? Perhaps not, in terms of the clear requirements I have discussed in this book. But certainly, we can see that the conscious breathing, the (unspoken) words of reconciliation, and the presence of a witnessing community (the analyst) served, for this highly introverted man, as authentic components of this particular mode of ritual.

Many significant life-cycle and lifestyle transitions are "ritually neglected" by our postmodern society. Life-cycle changes that often go unmarked include the ending of a nonmarital relationship, employment termination, health crises, and major surgery, to name a few. Loss is, at best, a doorway into something new. Ritual is a threshold allowing passage into this new experience, acting as a container for all the pieces of the "not yet."

There are a number of diseases or unexpected occurrences (e.g., cancer, dementia, trauma, heart attack, stroke, or diabetes) as a result of which our health and well-being can be compromised temporarily, or possibly forever. Ritually acknowledging this painful reality within a circle of family and friends can be liberating and supportive. Major surgery that leaves the body scarred or permanently changed (e.g., mastectomy, hysterectomy, prostate surgery, or amputation) might be seen as poignant moments for the ritual expression of loss. The purpose of ritual is to change our thoughts and feelings about a particular situation.

In the area of work and careers, rituals can serve to sustain people within organizations during times of work-related transitions that require letting go and moving on. Several years ago, the Harris Corporation staged an enormous New Orleans-style wake to mark the closure of a water-fabrication plant. Such a ritual, while it does not take away the pain of loss, does serve to engage those involved as full participants in the change, instead of rendering them helpless onlookers (Wall and Ferguson, 120). Sometimes, after having participated in a powerful ritual, we might still have a need to acquire a tangible reminder of the new direction upon which we have embarked. This tangible reminder might take the form of a plaque bearing a significant quote or perhaps the insignia of the new employer. Because we often tend to define ourselves by our work, any job change presents the opportunity for ritual. At such a time, we might find ourselves reconnecting with our priorities and goals in life.

Retirement is yet another lifestyle change that presents a clear opportunity for a transitional ritual in the workplace. Most retirement events, however, consist merely of entertaining ceremonies filled with words and the handing over of what is generally a symbol without profound meaning, unaccompanied by any performative utterance. The shadow is rarely engaged, except perhaps through superficial humor that lacks the respect required for this important element. Finally, such ceremonies are usually imposed from above and lack the necessary investment of time and careful, focused participation on the part of the retiree. What would happen if the retiree and the organizational leadership came together to plan an authentic ritual (i.e., one containing all the elements generally lacking in these events as noted)? It would also include an investment of time and consciousness in choosing the appropriate symbol, gathering the stories, honoring the work and the person of the retiree, and articulating his or her future hopes and dreams. In this way, the ritual more authentically honors the retiree, the transitional process, and the organizational community itself.

What about the home? The sudden eruption into the home scene of a previously fully employed partner can put enormous stress on a marriage. This seems to be especially true when it is the husband retiring from full-time work. The expectations of the two partners can be poles apart. He may take it for granted that he is now on permanent vacation, while often the wife is thinking "here comes another pair of hands to share the household chores."

One way of addressing this change might be to develop a ritual process whereby both partners share their perspectives, expectations, and hopes. These discussions would be the clear naming of the conflicting emotions in this transitional stage, thus preparing the way for a ritual action of mutual commitment to a new way of being together in retirement. The ritual could take the form of both parties speaking some performative words as they sign a written covenant drawn up within the framework of their discussions. The couple might choose to perform the ritual in a family gathering accompanied by a celebratory glass of champagne. The beauty of such an intimate ritual is that it comes from the hearts of the participants themselves, rather than being imposed from outside.

The ritual honoring of miscellaneous anniversaries of losses in family life can offer the opportunity for further healing and deeper intimacy, as these are liminal moments of transition. Anniversaries of the death of a loved one, the finalization of divorce, or even of a residence change, if the latter had carried a sense of loss, are significant examples of such moments. Punctuating the life journey with rituals and ritualizing behaviors seems to give order and meaning to life.

Rituals generally play a powerful role in helping us to move through, or resolve, our problems. Because ritual embraces liminal space and paradoxical truths, it has the ability to hold the tension of the opposites until something new is created in the individual psyche. For example, a number of years ago, Samantha, a client of mine, was struggling with a seesawing emotional struggle that left her depleted of energy and emotionally stranded between life choices and relational struggles. She had endured two automobile accidents, the loss of a long-term relationship, and termination from her job, all within a year or so. Unable to summon the desire or the will to go on with her life, she contemplated suicide. She wanted to die. As I listened to the seemingly unending litany of her pain, I knew intuitively that ritual might well help her move beyond this depressing place. She chose a funereal-style ritual, complete with a small coffin. At the chosen site, Samantha dug a hole into which she placed the coffin, containing several significant items related to her old life, reciting some short prayers over the "grave." She had brought with her two vases of flowers. One was placed beside the resting place of the coffin, symbolizing the death of the old; the other vase was taken home and placed in a prominent spot to affirm the promise of new life. This inclusive ritual, for Samantha, held together her endings and beginnings and assisted her to take the next steps in her life. Whether it is an interior conflict or a conflicted relationship between persons or groups, ritual can do much to bring healing and reconciliation. Samantha came to realize that instead of literally letting go of her life, she needed to accomplish this symbolically.

This story reminds me of the ritual release of the many demons from the man in Gerasa (Mark 5:1–20). Here was a person, like Samantha, tormented by many negative demons of self-deprecation who begged for relief. His demons, the dark and nasty voices of his interior disposition (both personal and communal), were cast into the animal world, so the evangelist tells us, where they disappeared into the depths of the healing underworld. Only when Jesus helped him to see that all these demonic voices needed to be contained somewhere else could he receive a modicum of peace and contentment over the chaos of his life. He was then reincorporated into the human community, enthusiastically sharing the story of his release.

In a more sinister scenario, victims of violence such as rape or robbery sometimes experience therapeutic ritual as a guiding light in the midst of their darkness of grief. This is the story of Lisa's healing. Several years ago, I participated in a wilderness retreat in which the retreatants were divided into teams—identified as "the hunters" and "the hunted." The hunted, designated "deer," were marked with various numbers or letters to identify them as prey, and each was given a chocolate candy bar, which, under the rules of the game, was a symbol of their "life." When a hunter drew close enough to identify the coded markings, the "deer" was required to halt and surrender to the hunter the candy bar representing his or her life. To the hunter belonged the choice—life or death. If the hunter returned the candy bar to the deer, he or she was free to live; if not, the deer was "killed" and could not continue in the game.

At the conclusion of the game, we gathered in the community room to process the experience. As the debriefing proceeded, it emerged that one of the participants, Lisa, a twenty-two-year-old single woman, had been raped the previous year. She was still struggling to come to terms with the violence perpetrated on her. During the unfolding of her story, she described her feelings when her "hunter" returned the candy bar to her; she experienced a powerful sense of life actually being given back to her in a dramatic way. What happened next was crucial. The retreat facilitator led Lisa to the outside balcony of the building, overlooking a valley. He motioned to the men in the room to follow. We gathered quietly behind Lisa as the facilitator helped her onto the balcony railing. He then invited her to let go and fall backward in a gesture of trust. Without looking at us, she fell backward into our arms. Holding her, we quietly, soothingly, rocked her back and forth, each man tenderly speaking affirming words to her, acknowledging her pain, but also inviting her to believe in the possibility of a healing masculine touch. These words were encapsulated by one man, who proclaimed in an intensely focused, if earthy manner: "See, not all men are jerks." This was powerful ritual for everyone present. And who would be surprised? Here were present all the elements required for authenticity of rites and transformational change:

- focused participation by everyone present
- the embodied ritual act of falling and being caught
- the central symbol of the balcony railing
- involvement of the shadow of societal and individual violence

- holding the tension of the opposites between past violation and future security with other men
- liminal space and time during a wilderness retreat

The result was an interior transformation on Lisa's part. This ritual occurred at the beginning of a two-week retreat. Lisa's demeanor and way of relating with others over the succeeding weeks were evidence of a dramatic change in her interior disposition.

Exilic departure from one's homeland, through choice or through economic/political necessity, is another difficult issue to address. This situation becomes even more complicated if the emigration is illegal, or is not sanctioned by family or friends. Perhaps the citizens of the new country are not welcoming, or prejudice is experienced in the neighborhood. Hostile or negative responses from the local population exacerbate the pain of separation/exile from one's homeland. For some people in a situation of exile, a ritual connected with their belief system or religion would carry a great deal of power. Symbols evocative of the homeland or religion can connect with their past; symbols from the new country of residence could serve to ground them in the present reality. Verbal expressions of conflicted feelings would be most appropriate, as would public mourning for the loss of the homeland. Perhaps, in this situation, there need to be separate rituals—one of separation from the homeland and one of incorporation into the new country. Caution needs to be exercised, however; sometimes a ritual can become overburdened by too much content—excessive wordiness or the presence of too many symbols or conflicting elements. The ritual then becomes more like a stew rather than an entrée into something new.

Facing the reality of the loss of a loved one, a family member, or even of a beloved pet, most people experience a time of great vulnerability and emotional distress—a situation in which ritual often can provide a unique space for safe and authentic expression of grief. Often, pregnancy ends in a miscarriage or stillbirth. Sometimes these life events cry out for some means of funerary expression to honor the loss experience. When a friend of mine, Rev. Ron Raab, CSC, was called in the middle of the night to a hospital for an urgent pastoral intervention, he was unprepared for what awaited him. He was escorted to a birthing room where a woman was weeping near the dead body of her infant son. Ron requested the assistance of the attending nurse, who in turn invited several other staff members to participate in an impromptu ritual. Ron began to sing a well-known, simple, haunting Christian refrain, over and over again, as the small group gathered together: "Jesus, remember me when you come into your kingdom / Jesus, remember me when you come into your kingdom." Here, in this place of death, Ron was proclaiming in song the life of the woman's faith. He gathered the dead infant into his arms, and after a few minutes, stepped forward and touched the woman's tear-stained cheeks. He then anointed the dead infant's forehead with his mother's tears. When the child was placed in her arms, she began once again to weep as the impromptu choir continued singing. Ron held this madonna and child close to his chest and then gave a blessing, with brief words of consolation. A simple, but healing, ritual.

It is good to recognize that the ending of life calls out for the same honor and respect as the beginning. It is not only the final moment of death, but the dying process itself, that ought to be honored. This can often be accidentally discovered by families who are narrowly focused on religious rites at the moment of death. In reality, there is a beautiful opportunity, where the dying process is gradual, for a profoundly moving ritual expression of gratitude, the sharing of memories, the honoring of the dying person's life, and loving farewells. So often, the beautiful and satisfying set of human pronouncements of the person's goodness is heard only at the funeral and not by the loved one during his or her lifetime. Ritual attention to the dying process can provide the vehicle for the dying person to hear the "eulogy" of his or her own goodness from those who loved him or her.

So far, the focus has been on the people surrounding the deathbed. How can we transform and give strength, courage, and consolation to the person who has entered the final stage of the dying process? Humanly speaking, there are a number of tasks to be accomplished by the person facing death; these tasks, although not mandatory, can help to prepare the way into a death that is serene and peaceful, with a sense of fulfillment and completion. Within this fragile landscape, ritual can provide a safe means of negotiating these delicate tasks, which generally might be categorized as:

- acknowledgments to be made
- "letting go's" to be accomplished
- litany of lasts to be celebrated (Anderson and Foley, 110)

Anderson and Foley, in their book *Mighty Stories, Dangerous Rituals: Weaving Together the Human and the Divine*, offer some helpful insights in this regard. The dying person may need to acknowledge unfulfilled tasks, dreams, achievements, limitations, and, perhaps especially, unresolved grievances and grudges. He or she may find the strength to consciously let go of old hostilities and lingering regrets, as well as the loving relationships that have supported him or her in life. Celebrating a "liturgy of lasts" might include a last dinner out, last lovemaking, a last visit to a favorite place, or a last time to leave the bedroom or hospital. The potential for the ritualization of all these tasks ought to be obvious. The limited range of physical actions available or possible for a dying person is certainly a factor to be considered; often, ritual actions in this area will be of a more passive variety and may, of necessity, be more verbal than physical in nature. Actions might include writing or dictating a life testament or autobiography, creating a taped or videoed "last message" for those left behind, sharing memories with loved ones while perusing photograph albums, writing letters of gratitude or reconciliation, or distributing beloved possessions as gifts; even planting a tree might be appropriate. The delicate dance of word and action in these rituals has the potential to create a healing and fulfilling conclusion to a person's life.

Sometimes the dying process can be trapped in a clinical setting—most obvious in a situation where artificial life support is to be withdrawn. The challenge presented to the family is often overwhelming. The symbolic significance of the "umbilical" tubes is evocative of the umbilical cord of the womb, and their withdrawal can be a powerful and frightening moment for the loved ones. It might be helpful if a ritual could capture the link between the cutting of the umbilical cord that leads to a new realm of life at birth and the cutting of the medical "umbilical cord" leading to another new realm of life through death.

For those who remain, this healing, this conclusion, is usually ritualized in a funeral service. The work of grieving is often supported by carefully planned and sensitively conducted funeral rites, which address the needs of the mourners and the life of the deceased. It is not only the deceased, but those who remain, who find themselves in a time of transition, the irreversible crossing over from one reality to another. For this reason, it is important that the funeral rites serve the process of mourning and not the demands of efficiency.

In the Catholic Church, the accompanying liturgical rites are generally contained in a three-step process, mirroring the life, death, and resurrection of Jesus Christ, by celebrating and honoring the life, death, and resurrection of the human person. Against the backdrop of the Sacred Scriptures, an evening vigil service celebrates the life of the deceased. The graveside service, with its formal ceremony, is centered on the body of the deceased, honoring the reality of the physical death. The funeral Mass, ritually situated as it is between these two ceremonies, honoring life and honoring death, functions as a bridge to the hope of the resurrection and new life. How does it do that?

In this eucharistic celebration, the story of the deceased is situated within the larger Christian story, and the promise and hope of resurrection are renewed in the presence of the gathered community of witnesses. The promise is recalled through the ritual action of the offering/surrender of one's life for divine transformation.

This tripartite division reflects van Gennep's idea of separation (from the living), initiation (into eternity), and reincorporation (into the larger cosmos). The three-part process allows for a more expansive ritual response, which can include, in its larger scope, the use of symbols, the weaving of stories of the life of the deceased, and the silences that are sometimes needed by people caught in inexpressible grief. Often there is a temptation to overload a single funeral event with too many words. This is where the three-part process is a useful framework for containing all these needs that would constitute more than a single ritual might bear. Some situations might call for a celebratory meal in which the stories could be continued and laughed and cried over. The Irish recognized this need and bequeathed to the world the wonderful tradition of the wake.

This tripartite division is seen very clearly in the story of Lazarus in the Christian Scriptures (John 11:1–44). When Jesus is summoned by Martha and Mary, their brother, Lazarus, is quite ill. He is already in transition to death. When his death occurs, he is in separation from the community he has known in life. With Jesus' performative words of exhortation, "Lazarus, come out!" Lazarus is called out of death into a new, fuller life. He is initiated into a more complete experience of his humanity; he has caught a glimpse of the larger picture; he has seen behind the veil of death. Lazarus is then returned to the community with the words: "Unbind him, and let him go." This is a wonderful example of the community reincorporating the individual.

Funerals are sometimes a starting point for a grieving process that can take two years or more to complete. Ritual actions can continue, therefore, to support us in the ongoing process. These can consist of setting aside daily grieving periods in a special place, or ritualizing certain behavior with objects symbolically linked to the deceased, or creating personal symbols of our relationship to the deceased (e.g., poetry, artwork, music, or sculpture). Months or even years after the funeral we might feel a further need to create a personal ritual or another memorial to the deceased as a means of moving through the grieving process.

Several years ago, during a pastoral mission in Australia, I heard the story of an older woman (who had no religious faith), who had buried her husband's ashes in her rose garden near her clothesline—a spot in her garden that she visits daily to hang up her clothes. She greets him each time, has a few words about her day, the children, and occasionally pulls up a lawn chair and sits and has what she calls "a nice cup of tea" while she remembers their love and reminisces. This struck me as quite a healthy piece of ritualizing behavior for her.

With each phase of grief, perhaps, a different ritual could be created. However, there are particular problems or challenges that we face when beginning such a process. Living within a society that is ritually impoverished, we may not know or understand the elements of effective ritual, or have the resources to proceed. There is also the danger of an individual's ritual leading to separation rather than a deeper immersion into the community. Of course, this might have particular application in the case of a bereaved person.

Death rituals help us to resist the disintegrating face of grief by offering a socially acceptable framework of expression. They provide a format for the vocalization of feelings of sadness, guilt, anger, dread, and fear. These rituals also allow the living to feel useful and connected to the dead through a structured format that reduces the confusion, helplessness, and isolation of the mourners (Gordon, 85). The gift of good ritual is its ability to help us to not only express and contain our grief, but also to incorporate it into the larger tapestry of our life.

Losses are a necessary part of life. They are timely opportunities to create intimate rituals of healing, reconciliation, and mourning to assist in the process of integration and forward movement. It is here in the dark aspects of reality that we discover what is most important to each of us. Ritual assists us in expressing our thoughts and feelings in ways that can change our life and bring us greater happiness.

Questions for Personal Reflection:

- What individual losses in my life need to be acknowledged and ritually let go in order for me to move forward?

- What particular anniversaries of family and friends might I ritually celebrate as a means of honoring their lives?
- How can I better prepare for my own death or that of a loved one?

Questions for Parish Leaders:

- How might parish staff members be more sensitive and creative in responding to the needs of parishioners for ritual expression at important junctures in their lives? What are some possible ways of honoring the losses in people's lives?
- How might we as a parish ritually prepare the living for dying and the dying for living eternally? What can we do as individuals, parish teams, and a community?

Tips for Parish Leaders:

- Involve people working in teams of expertise (e.g., dying process, grief counseling, funeral planning, grief support group).
- Connect persons with similar losses (e.g., cancer survivors, victims of violence, addicts in recovery, widows).
- Consult with ritual specialists.

7

Holidays, Public and Religious Events: Celebration or Chaos?

IN NORTH AMERICAN society, holidays can present annual occasions for reconnection with family, friends, and the traditions of the community. On Christmas, Valentine's Day, Thanksgiving, New Year's Day, Martin Luther King, Jr., Day, Easter, July Fourth, or Labor Day, people usually have the day off from work and daily routines are suspended to allow some acknowledgment of the cultural celebration. Traditions prescribed by our family of origin or culture often dictate the day's unfolding or events. Specially prepared foods, clothing, or activities contribute to the process of reconnecting with loved ones. Holidays, however, can be a time when we experience excessive family tension and anxiety. Psychiatrist Evan Imber-Black ascribes this tension to "a combination of high expectations, extra work, memories of previous holidays, and long-standing relationship strains that have not been successfully addressed" (260). Further, she notes, "[A] family's greatest strengths and its most painful vulnerabilities are generally in the air at holiday time" (260).

Some people may also experience societal or family pressure regarding the manner, the accoutrements, or even the timing of celebrations. Often, too, holidays can produce stresses in common familial relationships when people are torn between two or more households. The practice of different generations gathering at these times sometimes highlights the differences in expectations of particular holiday observances, especially religious services. With sensitive planning and discussion beforehand, it may be that ritual could bring about the connectedness that the family might need or desire. In this situation, as in others already discussed, ritual can function to bring about order and direction to people's lives.

These differences, harnessed by an appropriate ritual, actually offer many possibilities for reenvisioning certain family traditions so that they remain alive for the family. This is especially true if there has been a recent death in the family around the holidays, and the tradition was strongly associated with that person. A living family tradition is meaningful for as long as it speaks to the present reality of the celebrating community. If people are celebrating a particular tradition disconnected from the present context of their lives, then that tradition eventually becomes brittle or two-dimensional; it will not stand the test of time.

Thoughtful preparation is an essential prerequisite for meaningful holiday celebrations. This allows the participants to decide for themselves what is most important about a particular celebration. Welcoming input from each family member, or from the different sectors of the community, keeps the story of the group vibrant and alive. That story will then have an immense effect on the way the ritual plays out. Even with the pressure to conform to outdated societal customs or family traditions, personalizing the ritual is a crucial step. Imber-Black relates the example of a Jewish couple appalled by the crass commercialization of Christmas, which was affecting their children's expectations for the Hanukkah celebration. Their response was to

> intentionally organize each of the eight nights of Hanukkah around a theme that would move it

away from a copy of Christmas, strung out over eight nights. So, with their three young children, they now have Homemade Presents Night, Food and Fire Night, Music Night, Book and Story Night, and Tzedakah (charity) Night. They focus on Jewish songs, games, foods, and stories each night, so Hanukkah can take on its own definition. (234)

Authenticity demands that families write their own reality into these holiday celebrations. An illustration: Sarah and Bill Langston's two teenage sons had recently started their first jobs and were captivated by the stories of the early history of Labor Day. The boys wanted to make the holiday more interesting, so they decided to research its history in the United States. On the morning of the holiday, the boys shared their research by reading aloud to each other portions of the history. They then interviewed their parents about their first work experiences. They were surprised to discover that their father had worked in an ice-cream parlor and their mother had picked blueberries. Their conversation turned to the meaning of labor and the making of wise career choices. The Langstons concluded the day by going to the store to buy all the necessary ingredients to make old-fashioned blueberry sundaes for dessert to celebrate the boys' deeper understanding of their place in the work force (Imber-Black, 236–37).

This family celebration became alive and meaningful because everyone was a participant, and everyone contributed by telling their own story about work. Thus, they ritualized the boys' entry into the labor force, adopting a symbol, powerful in the memory of that family—blueberry sundaes. Here the work experiences of the two parents were integrated into one central symbol. Time and place were bridged in a ritual designed to move forward the next generation.

Sensitivity is needed when two or more families are celebrating the holidays in two or more households. One household might host Thanksgiving dinner, while another hosts dessert; or the family could celebrate the holiday on two separate days. While the reality of the calendar is always strong, it is sometimes possible and appropriate to exercise flexibility in the timing of gatherings, according to the needs of the family or community structure. I know of one family in which the husband works as an offshore oil-rig operator and is at sea for two weeks at a time. Each year, the family plans their Christmas celebration around his work schedule. This has the added bonus for the married children; now they can spend Christmas day with their in-laws.

Holidays can cause issues of family discontent, loss, and separation to surface. If the emotional intensity surrounding the absence of a missing parent, a deceased relative, or a major change in family status is ignored, the situation can only worsen. This is especially pertinent for children, as they feel a lack of control over the events. Perhaps before the holidays begin, the family could gather to discuss the missing relative, share treasured memories, look at pictures of the relative, or encourage the child to write a letter to him or her. With the benefit of these preparatory exercises, the family might then be able to create a ritual to help them contain and sustain the conflicting emotions around their experience of loss and change.

Holidays have tremendous potential for facilitating healing and making new connections. They can provide opportunities to use the same symbols or action elements in order to create a vibrant new meaning. For example, in one blended family, people were asked to name a favorite dish that they wanted included in the Thanksgiving meal. Another blended family took the idea of Thanksgiving a step further, by inviting each member to fill out a "thanks" card on which each person wrote a message of appreciation about every other member. Before they sat down to eat, they read aloud these affirmations. In this way, they were making symbolic connections that did not yet exist in practice.

Religious holidays present a unique challenge, especially if any family member has changed belief systems or ecclesial allegiances. One way to ease the tension around these days is to begin a conversation months ahead of the event, to secure a common ground of celebration. Perhaps the family can honor and witness each person's faith or spiritual experience in singular ways during the day. The question to consider might be: Is there a communal symbol sufficiently multivocal to contain the significance of the day and the family relationship? If we ground the discussion in the true fundamental essence of healthy religion—which is a binding-together function—it might be possible to develop some appropriate religious rituals for the family. This presents an obvious challenge in the pluralistic society in which we live and needs to be approached with great sensitivity. But the absence of good ritual and conscious awareness can leave a family or community with empty, repetitive behaviors that do nothing to assist the family's maturation process or search for meaning. For example, at every birthday gathering, Uncle Bob has to tell a joke, or a specific relative has to carve the turkey, or the whole family must watch a certain television program. The result can be an emotional impasse, which will manifest itself in various negative ways in the family structure.

Moving from the family to the public sphere, it is possible to show that rituals can play a significant role in the life and culture of a corporation. Change and transition are built into corporate life with mergers, downsizing, or expansion into new fields through acquisitions presenting a daunting task for the ritualist to find a metaphorical way to express the associated human anxiety. Deal and Kennedy assert:

A corporate culture—and the values it embodies—
must be ritualized and celebrated if it's going to
thrive…without expressive events, any culture will
die. In the absence of ceremony or ritual, important values have no impact. Ceremonies are to the
culture what the movie is to the script, the concert
is to the score, or the dance is to values that are difficult to express in any other way. (63)

I know that a number of large multinational organizations recognize this need and specifically incorporate ritual
expression into their day-to-day operations. In corporate life,
as in family and community life, rituals can help to bring
meaning and order where there is change and chaos.

In recent years, parish closures have become a relatively
new experience for the Catholic Church in the United States.
Caused by financial necessity or lack of clergy, these closures
represent a disturbing and painful transition for the groups of
the believers involved. Once again, chaos, loss, and dispersion
could be ameliorated through a sound ritual process addressing both the endings of an old community and the assimila-
tion of the group into a new parish. This has been done with
significantly good results in some areas of the country.

In the larger arena of the global community, peoples
and nations struggle to live responsibly and yet comfortably
on our fragile planet. Massive environmental changes—
global warming, rain-forest destruction, species depletion,
and water pollution—are sources of deep concern in a society struggling to balance the need for development with sus-
tainable growth. In this arena, where the whole world is the
stage, the scale and the public display dimension of ritual
enter a new realm. Here Ronald Grimes's survey of the complex framework and accoutrements available to ritual plan-
ners is a useful reminder of the possibilities in the public

ritual arena. He lists eleven components of good ritual and gives examples of each:

Component	Example
Actions:	dancing, walking, kneeling
Places:	shrines, sanctuaries
Times:	holidays, seasons, eras
Objects:	fetishes, masks, icons, costumes
Groups:	congregations, sects, moieties, nations
Figures and roles:	gods, ancestors, priests, shamans
Qualities, quantities:	circularity, seven, red
Language:	myths, stories, texts, orations
Sounds:	music, songs, chants
Attitudes:	beliefs, intentions, belief in ritual efficacy, thankfulness
Emotions:	ecstasy (*Rite Out of Place*, 109)

This multidimensional approach to ritual seems especially important when the scale is national or global.

The aspirations of any healthy society will center on social coherence. The essential elements of this ideal state include forgiveness and reconciliation, the healing of societal grief, integration of all its members, internal solidarity, and an authentic sense of identity. In the search for these necessary movements in a society, ritual can be a powerful engine for driving the often-difficult processes. In a story of a search for authentic forgiveness and reconciliation, Herbert Anderson describes such a ritual:

> It was mid-December 1972. The negotiations between the United States and North Vietnamese delegations in Paris had collapsed, and President Nixon had renewed the order for massive bomb-

ing of Hanoi and Haiphong. U.S. citizens, already horrified by the war, were stunned at the brutality of this sudden and violent re-escalation. In one small church in Milwaukee, an interdenominational group of Christians gathered in a reconciliation service to pray for forgiveness and ask for absolution. The ritual that occurred that winter's eve, however, was like no other they had ever experienced.

"We beg for forgiveness," they prayed, "for our sin against humanity, and for the violence our country perpetrates in our name." A lone minister, obviously of oriental descent, garbed in alb and stole, answered back from the sanctuary, "Your words are empty; your actions betray you; the murdering continues."

"We are truly repentant," the assembly continued, "for our national arrogance, for our reliance on bombs rather than God, and for our thirst for war rather than peace." The minister replied, "Your words are easy, but they are hollow to the thousands of innocents you have savaged in the name of democracy."

"We ask for absolution," the people prayed. "Absolve us for the pain and destruction we rain on the people of North Vietnam, and for our inability to stop the leaders who commit these crimes in our name." A pause...and then frightful, unexpected words from the minister: "I deny you absolution; I withhold the consolation of the church from you; I refuse to collaborate in your search for spiritual comfort, for though you may be repentant, you have not been reconciled with your enemies." (Anderson and Foley, 169)

This poignant story reminds us that reconciliation is neither as easy nor as accessible as we would like it to be, nor is absolution automatic, even when repentance is authentic. This minister intended to shock the assembly into new attitudes and actions. He did this by denying them the expected ritual of absolution. In his view, the necessary engagement with the shadow, on the part of the assembled faithful, had not taken place; they were seeking comfort and release, but the minister was inviting them into a transformative response. Movement forward could not take place until reconciliation was linked to repentance.

Premature forgiveness and reconciliation can sometimes abort the healing process by denying or papering over the real causes of suffering. Authentic reconciliation is not about forgetting; it is about remembering in a new way. Reconciliation involves the acceptance of contradictions in the hope that the redeeming paradox will be discovered. Ritual is a privileged place for appropriating this redeeming narrative by exploring the darkness of the communal psyche and the naming of its internal demons. Such communal gatherings have a unique capacity for acknowledging and embracing personal and social tales of violence and destruction.

For example, in the context of the Arab-Israeli situation, rituals are an important resource for small-scale conflict resolution. These indigenous rituals of reconciliation contain the following elements:

- They emerge from the grass roots community ties and cultural patterns of Middle Eastern society (witnessing community).
- The two parties involved are brought together by a third party, with the meeting taking place on neutral ground (liminal space).

- The parties acknowledge and name the issue of painful conflict (the shadow is engaged).
- Apologies are exchanged (performative words).
- Compensation is decided and symbolic gifts are exchanged (symbolic action).
- The parties join in forgiveness and reconciliation (developmental change and transformation occurs). (Irani, 141–44)

Perhaps the very authenticity of these rituals has brought about success where the United States and the international community have failed. Success might be small in scale, but it is real. With this model in mind, the United States might have an opportunity to reframe its role in the Mideast as an active facilitator "helping to empower peoples in the region to develop culturally relevant models of reconciliation, democracy, and development. This would help to ameliorate perceived tensions between modernity and tradition, as well as between secularism and religion" (Irani, 145).

A process that sometimes is not recognized as ritual but carries the power and the authority of authentic ritual is the implementation of restorative justice through a truth commission. The truth commission represents a conscious ritual event in which victims are enabled to "find their voice," to publicly confront their tormentors, and to acquire necessary information about the atrocities committed. The success of truth commissions in South Africa and South America attests to the power of this ritual collective healing process. Genocide, mass killings, or intense civil wars present a formidable task for a society needing to move beyond its trauma to healing and reconciliation. Only the pursuit of truth will provide the basis of healing and reconciliation. Grieving rituals, public rituals of reconciliation, and public covenants emanating from such work can continue to foster this process of healing. Perhaps the traditional call to a lamentation ritual in these circumstances might be appropriate. Jeremiah 6:26 reminds us of this ancient ritual expression of deep grief and mourning, which includes fasting, weeping, and the use of ashes.

Soldiers returning home from armed conflict need ceremonies and rituals to help facilitate their transition back into peaceful society. Traditionally, what has occurred has been ceremony rather than ritual—generally consisting of such elements as welcoming home at the airport by local or national dignitaries, triumphant marches down Main Street, flag-waving, and speeches. There was no hint of the shadow; only the celebration of honor and glory. In the past, these ceremonies traditionally may have acted as a cooling-down process for hearts afire with war and violence. However, in contemporary society, there is a paradoxical need to reaffirm and validate the men and women returning from politically unpopular wars. Why? Because, in this situation, there is a social need to:

- help contain the polarity of emotions for both the returning soldiers and society
- assist society and the individual soldiers to acknowledge the pain of the past in the present situation, with hope for a better world
- name the shadow of the politically unpopular war; such a war leaves people's lives torn open physically, emotionally, and spiritually

Here, ritual, with its functions of ordering of life, bridging the shadow and the persona, facilitation of transition, and enrichment of community, may well have a significant role to play. Symbols are important components of ritual because they bridge the historical and the geographical, and hold power and energy simultaneously (e.g., an eighty-two-year-old Army veteran holds the U.S. flag in the present moment: The memory of a battle in 1942 merges with the pride of the present moment and future hope for his country. Guadalcanal, Los Angeles, and his country become one. Time and place merge in an emotional congruence of tremendous power, which he himself is unable to explain.)

What happens when a community, in fact, does not wish to reembrace the returning warriors into itself? In 1979, in Anaheim, California, at the Catholic Religious Education Congress, an unplanned, yet extraordinary ritual took place that addressed this very situation. It changed lives forever.

Elisabeth Kübler-Ross, during a workshop on stages of grief, talked about the need to ritualize the process of grieving. At one point she invited, almost by chance, any Vietnam veterans present to stand and identify themselves. Three did, but almost immediately one lost courage and fled the room. He was persuaded to return, and all three stood in the center of the assembly. She then asked all present to form a circle surrounding the three men and to sing "America the Beautiful," followed by "The Star Spangled Banner." In this poignant moment, she invited all of those present—irrespective of their political leaning or their feelings about the Vietnam conflict—who had lost a loved one in that war to come forward. The invitation was to thank these men for their contribution, the thanks being expressed in whatever way felt comfortable—verbal expression, a hug, a handshake, or even just silent touch. At the conclusion of this honoring ritual, Kübler-Ross turned to the veterans and asked, "Now, how do you feel?" In the midst of his tears, one of the three men walked up to the microphone and thanked the gathering from the depths of his heart:

"I did not want to go to this war," he said, " I was only eighteen, and I was more afraid of going to jail than I was of going to war. When I returned home after my tour of duty, I was not prepared for the reception that awaited me. People treated me like a stranger, or even worse—like the enemy. I didn't feel like I belonged anymore. But today I feel as though, for the first time, I have been welcomed back home."

This is a classic case of the community not reembracing the warrior. For these three returning warriors, but only for these three, this ritual brought healing and integration.

In an increasingly violent and unsafe world, it is essential that we create communal and societal rituals for individuals and groups that have suffered the effects of social violence in order to dissipate any further desire for violence or revenge. No examination of the need for societal rituals would be complete without a penetrating look at our society's response to the events of September 11, 2001. The world has changed forever, and we had better learn how to deal with the new realities of terrorist attacks, and the fact that civilians, not soldiers, constitute the largest mass of victims of martial and political violence. As a nation, our expression of grief and anger in response to the carnage of the World Trade Center attack failed to bring significant healing, reconciliation, or social coherence. A form of internal solidarity was certainly achieved, but its appropriateness was questionable, especially in the eyes of the rest of the world. Why was this? It was obvious that people were looking for some kind of grieving ritual or lamentation to contain their collective grief and anger. As a relative of a victim, I was disappointed—in fact, appalled—at the simplistic ritualizing response to this tragedy. It seemed to consist mostly of waving U.S. flags and lighting candles. Neither action did anything to assuage my grief; they seemed, for many people, to serve only to fan the fires of revenge and retributive justice. Here is a prime example, at a societal level, of a community's failure to understand the need for well-thought-out and authentic ritual. In the absence of enlightened political and religious leadership, people can be caught in the most simplistic form of symbolic expression of solidarity and ritualizing display. No attention is paid to the necessary elements for effective ritual; there is no transformation of the conflicted issues. Rather, the minimalistic symbol becomes the driving force of expression, with no resolution emerging. The ubiquitous flag displays became a means of perpetuating the negative emotions; the symbol became self-serving, not liberating. There is more to the recovery from disaster than the seeking of comfort and solidarity.

New situations require ritual creativity and imagination. At a personal level, I have tried to find a response to meet this need. In June 2005, I visited the World Trade Center site with my friend, Father Richard Kelly, OMI. We made a pilgrimage to this secular shrine and found ourselves making an impromptu "stations of the cross," a Catholic devotional practice in which the participants honor the various stages along the way of Jesus' final suffering and death. I wanted to see Ground Zero with my own eyes and be reconciled with my anger and shock at such violence. I wanted to put the memory of this event in historical perspective in order to move forward. We decided to walk around the entire site (liminal space), pausing to read the names of the deceased, the explanations and statistics concerning the event. Walking was our central symbolic action, and I felt grounded and connected with the present moment, journeying with the memory of the dead and with those still living, trying to create something new from the ashes of destruction. As I walked in silence, praying and reflecting, I

103

felt a spirit of heaviness or burden that was bigger than the North American pain itself. It was a share in the cosmic human tragedy of loss.

As we concluded our walk around the site, I viewed the architectural plans for the future of the site and felt a sense of hope for something new and better in a violent world. Walking away from the site and the witnessing community of the construction workers and police officers, I took several deep breaths and then stepped away into the flow of traffic. I felt as though I had finally put to rest a dark, ominous spirit that had haunted my heart. I felt a combination of awe at such overwhelming darkness, and yet a sense of acceptance. I finally recognized that there is no satisfactory explanation for evil, that it is endemic to the human situation. Bewilderment, horror, and anger were transformed into a level of acceptance. The liminal space created a place for us to enter into the realization of the enduring presence of evil in the human situation. The symbolic action of walking in silence embodied my desire to walk with the victims. Performative words were replaced with a focused, attentive silence. I felt the conscious presence of a witnessing community in the persons of Father Richard and the on-site police officers and construction workers. Authentic ritual had taken place.

But what about for our nation? Grimes offers a thoughtful social commentary on disaster of this sort:

> In the face of a disaster, with whom is it most urgent to express solidarity—"fellow countrymen" or the planet? In the face of disaster, what subtexts seep from beneath pious declarations uttered in public? There is not only acute danger in disasters (towers falling, planes dropping, floods rising, wars breaking out) but also the chronic danger of ritually sanctioned self-righteousness. The danger in rituals is that they can underwrite a desperate

obsession with declaratives and imperatives: The truth is....The truth shall be....The danger is that disaster rituals can buttress an impatience with questions and an unwillingness to abide with ambiguity or uncertainty. (86)

Have we, as a nation, learned to use ritual as an agent of transformation? Or have we decided that we prefer a cosmetic solution? Several years after the event of September 11, the national response to the devastation of Hurricane Katrina seemed to indicate that we have a way to go in learning to engage in a healthy way with our society's shadow in our approach to public ritual. The Christian churches, and specifically the Catholic Church, must pay similar attention to the need for authentic ritual to heal the immense suffering caused by a different kind of violence—the criminal abusive behavior of some of the clergy. This might offer healing and reconciliation and enable movement forward within and between individuals. Ritual can be a powerful tool for binding, healing, or reconciling in the hands of an individual, a family, a community, or a nation when the vicissitudes of life, relationships, change, and trauma are to be faced with courage, determination, and hope for the future.

Questions for Personal Reflection:

- How might I improve my holiday celebrations by using ritual expressions?
- Are there particular religious holidays where rituals might help in the family celebration?
- Might ritual assist me in expressing and containing my own anger, fear, anxiety, or helplessness about national/international tragedies or natural disasters?

Questions for Pastoral Leaders:

- How might the parish staff create rituals for the celebration of public holidays and religious events that can deepen the meaning and significance of the event?
- What types of rituals are needed for the welcoming home and integration of military personnel?
- How can we create rituals of healing and reconciliation for the victims of clergy abuse? For employees caught in the midst of corporate mergers? For those grappling with the fallout of national/international tragedies or natural disasters?

Tips for Pastoral Leaders:

- Involve the larger community in the research, planning, and participation of the ritual process.
- Notice the topics of conversations, the worries, anxieties that keep surfacing at different levels in parish life and plan rituals accordingly. Especially in times of economic hardship, with job losses, home foreclosures, and even families uprooted, we need to look for ways to help our people make difficult transitions.
- Dedicate a certain evening once a month to ritual expression of a particular topic or issue.
- Begin a parish meeting with a simple ritual as a catechetical tool to model for others how to do it.
- Create a series of lamentation rituals to be used in times of social grief and mourning.

8

What If It Doesn't Work for Me? Getting It Right

SOME QUARTERS OF our postmodern society regard rituals with varying degrees of ridicule, distrust, and disbelief. Perhaps this is because of some impoverished experiences of ritual, a misunderstanding of a ritual's purpose, or a failed ritual experience. In some areas of society, rituals have been unfairly linked with unhealthy religious practices. Without meaningful rituals at their disposal, people often create shallow rituals from ceremonies or instill disproportionate meaning into events and objects. For example, we often see this in the areas of big-league sports and sporting memorabilia.

Sometimes a ritual fails in its goal of transformation. What then? Since ritual is a complex phenomenon, it can fail in numerous ways. British ritualist, J. L. Austin, in a wonderful turn of phrase, lists nine such "infelicitous performances" (see Appendix B). Perhaps the ritual was successful on the social level but failed empirically. It is helpful to assess and evaluate the ritual experience with objective questions in order to get at the root cause of failure.

Who decides or determines that a ritual has failed? I believe that the determination is in the result. Has there been authentic transformation on the part of the participant(s)? If not, then there has been a failure on some level of the ritual enactment. It is rare for a ritual to fail on all levels or phases of the event. I would suggest that the ritual practitioner take a searching look at what went wrong. Perhaps the following questions might be helpful in uncovering the reason for the failure: Was the focus of the ritual proper too broad or unclear? Were there too many symbols or words that diffused the energy of concentration? Was the shadow honestly engaged, or was there, instead, more effort on making the ritual look "nice" or "perfect"? Was there a sufficient investment of time and emotional awareness in planning, reflecting, and discussing the ritual? Did the witnessing community validate the ritual?

Troubleshooting Ritual Failures

The ritual didn't work.

It is possible that the goal of a ritual might be too large or overladen with excessive emotion, and therefore needs to be broken down into smaller goals, with different rituals powering the movement of transformation forward. Perhaps more emotional unpacking of the underlying issues is needed in the preparation stage. A good example of this occurred when a Catholic bishop asked a focus group to plan a ritual addressing the clergy abuse scandal. The group informed him that it would take several rituals over a lengthy period to facilitate the complex processes of lamenting, healing, and reconciling. These separate but interrelated issues could not be integrated into a single ritual. Remember, quality of execution, not quantity of actions or words, is important here.

The participants are not actively engaged in the process.

The attitude with which one enters a ritual action is key to opening the interior life to the possibility of transformation. Focused attention is essential. There is no special magic formula for ritual. The ritual provides the place and the opportunity for the person to be actively transformed. Perhaps the planned ritual is too lengthy and needs to be tightened up or shortened; or the chosen space and time are inappropriate for the desired ritual. I remember one initiation ritual that began at 3 a.m. as a means of instilling the importance of the lesson. The participants never forgot it. In some circumstances and for some people, repeating the ritual or re-creating another ritual for a later date can assist in the process of positive transformation. This repetitive ritual can then strengthen the interior healing work of the practitioner.

The ritual is tepid, with no real power.

If the ritual is too *polite* or *nice*, it is often a sign that the shadow is not involved. Perhaps the participants need to introduce an aspect of play or humor into the ritual space (cf. the menopause ritual in chapter 4), choose a more multivocal symbol, or choose a person who will represent the shadow in an expressive way. In many of the Native American tribes, the trickster played this role, pointing out in amusing ways the foibles and shortcomings of the tribe. The clown or jester is a more traditional, though very tame form of this role in Western cultural behavior. Rituals ground us in the present experience and, for the most part, help us avoid impulsive activity and compulsive self-restriction, so that our behavior can be humanized and sanctified. In some cases, rituals seek to elicit such behavior to allow for a cathartic release. For this reason, rituals often have an element of play or creativity and therefore engage the inner child archetype.

There are too many words in the ritual space.

Use words sparingly and only if necessary in ritual space. Too many words can be an escape from the real purpose of ritual—to engage with the deeper desire of the soul. The preparation and planning phase of the ritual event is the time to air one's thoughts and feelings in a way that can focus and contain the performative words of the ritual action. One of the intriguing aspects of ritual is that its language is evocative rather than descriptive; thus, there is an actual power in the words spoken. The words are meant to be few, spoken with clarity and purpose, as a means of transformation.

There are too many symbols, with accompanying explanations.

Symbols speak for themselves. Their language is soulful and profound, eliciting reflection and response. Too many symbols flood the unconscious, or overwhelm one's thoughts and offer little means of focused response. A good measure of a meaningful symbol is to ask: "Is it multivocal? Does it speak to several layers and levels of the human experience?" Signs have one meaning; symbols have several meanings. Use fewer symbols to assist the process of the participants remembering the lesson learned. You might want to consult with a ritual specialist or trained professional for added insight.

The dramatic action is long on show and short on meaning.

Perhaps the action is disembodied, or the focus of the ritual is centered too much on the spoken words. The action could be too *tame* or *nice* for the participants. This is often so in the case of rituals for males. The dramatic action must be connected to the inner reality of the participants. Symbols are in the service of the ritual action (processing, digging, falling, etc.). The dramatic action must be intelligible and recognizable to the participants; otherwise, they will be left with the question: "What did that mean?" The focus then moves to the intellectual ruminations of trying to figure out the significance of the action rather than being immersed in the embodied transformative event. What are you seeking to celebrate, honor, or pass on to the participants? Make sure this is clear, concise, and congruent on all levels of expression. The acting out of the ritual reminds us to "live as if"—to bring the imaginal experience of ritual to the literal reality of our daily life. Our actions really do change the way we think and feel. We do not wait for something magical to drop from the sky; we must do the work ourselves. Follow-through after the ritual is complete is also a necessary component. Continuing to live in the new reality accentuates the lesson learned in ritual space and time and makes the change permanent.

There is a failure to provide the appropriate ambiance.

Creating the right time and space is a key component for the success of the ritual. Using the right combination of light, color, sound, and environment is very important for people. It heightens the sensual experience of the ritual event and makes it more memorable. Perhaps it would be helpful to consult with a ritualist or artistic person for some ideas on how to accomplish this.

Insincerity on the part of the participants defuses the effect of the ritual.

If the participants cannot enter the ritual space with a sincere, focused attitude, then the ritual should be delayed for another opportunity. This is serious business; a mature demeanor and attentive disposition are called for. Perhaps there still is more emotional unpacking needed before the individual(s) are ready to participate in the ritual.

The witnessing community is not present.

Invite at least one person to accompany you in the ritual expression. In the case of a vision quest, or similar solitary event where this is not possible, choose a person or group of persons who are willing to "hold the center" for you through prayer or meditation, and then welcome you back home for your reincorporation. The witnessing community is composed of one or more persons who vouch for and remind the ritual practitioner(s) of the reality of the ritual event. They act as a mirror or mnemonic device for the transformative experience, to assist the ritual practitioner from slipping back into the same old patterns of attitude and behavior. This is part of the necessary follow-through after the ritual event.

In the context of troubleshooting rituals, it could be useful to examine the phenomenon of rituals going awry, and thus exacerbating the situation for which they are seeking a resolution. A number of factors and circumstances might destroy the efficacy of a ritual, including relational factors in a group, situational content, lack of authentic intent, or emotional "distraction" because of a past traumatic event. In their book, *Rituals for Our Times: Celebrating, Healing, and Changing Our Lives and Our Relationships*, Evan Imber-Black and Janine Roberts describe some of the possibilities:

> The true purpose of the ritual may be distorted by shame....The person or the relationship for whom the ritual is intended may get lost in a flurry of elaborate preparations. The ritual may be overshadowed or intruded upon by a traumatic event that occurs close in time to the important life-cycle passage. Already troubled family relationships may overwhelm the ritual. Or the ritual may be unbalanced, reflecting the needs and desires of only one part of the family. (278)

This impoverished ritual experience can be very disconcerting for the ritual planner. The participant expects a transformational event to help him or her move forward and instead is confronted with a developmental step backward, which may have lasting negative consequences. The same authors observe that "many families date major relationship cut-offs and painful unresolved conflicts from interactions during life-cycle rituals. When a life-cycle ritual is recalled with pain and disappointment, subsequent rituals, such as birthdays, anniversaries, or holidays, are often interrupted or minimized" (278). We might identify, for example, a wedding ceremony dominated by the recent death of a parent, an ill-prepared divorce ritual where words and actions of recrimination and bitterness continue to flow, or a family holiday function in which one person dominates the proceedings by insisting that all his or her demands are met. For this reason, we should address the unhealed pain sooner rather than later. If the pain is not transformed, it will be transmitted in one form or another.

Sometimes simply repeating the ritual event—perhaps with a few minor changes—can be most helpful in responding to this pain or disappointment. I remember hearing of one World War II veteran who roundly complained each year that he had spent his twenty-first birthday in a foxhole in the Pacific arena of the war. Decades later, he still carried this disappointment within him. Finally, after hearing this story for the umpteenth time, the parish religious education coordinator decided that it was time to do something. Nothing new happens unless there is some type of intervention. Fortunately, the coordinator finally heard the real pain behind the complaint and decided to intervene. She set about planning a twenty-first birthday party complete with invitations, balloons, cake, ice cream, and even games. It was a great hit. Attendees enjoyed themselves and the veteran could finally say that he had received a "proper" twenty-first birthday party. Think of how this could be applied to aborted graduation ceremonies or events missed because of illness or accident. The possibilities are endless.

In the Christian Scriptures (Mark 8:22–26), we see Jesus repeating a ritual to heal a blind man, perhaps as a way of demonstrating this. The first time Jesus put spittle on the man's eyes, laid hands on him, and asked if he could see anything. The man replied, "I can see people, but they look like trees, walking." What went wrong? Why didn't the ritual "work"? We don't know. However, we do know that Jesus then laid hands on the blind man's eyes a *second time* and prayed. After this, the man could see perfectly; his sight was restored. We could also read this story symbolically; the man began to see in layers or stages, much as we often experience ourselves as growing in insight.

Sometimes the ritual process itself is derailed. Imber-Black and Roberts relate the story of an eleven-year-old boy whose father died of cancer. Because his mother and grandparents felt he was too young and impressionable, he did not attend the funeral. Without a real outlet for his pain, the boy began to build his life around an idealized image of his father, which eventually led him to some negative acting-out behavior. After several years, the boy and his mother finally entered therapy, where he discovered a respectful space to discuss his pent-up grief over his father's death, and his own subsequent response. With coaching from the therapist, the boy sought out family members to obtain more information about his father. On the eighth anniversary of his father's death, he planned a memorial service to which he invited family members. He planned the ritual itself, presided over it, and was able to complete his grieving in the bosom of his family. After participating in this transformative ritual, he returned to school and graduated (279–80).

If a ritual has been unsuccessful or the process has been derailed, as in this example, it is sometimes a good idea to create a new ritual so that relationships can be renewed and long-term anguish alleviated. Preparation for this type of ritual often requires a concentrated period of attention to the relationships and aspects of one's life that have been affected by the failed ritual.

Human beings daily make use of ritualized actions and words to assist them to organize their day and transition from one situation to another. These actions give a sense of order and power, as well as an attitude of contentment. Without these ritualizations, people often feel displaced or irritable. "As a particular act of ritualizing becomes more and more familiar, as it is repeated so often that it seems to circle round upon itself, it comes to seem less like a pathway and more like a shelter. These two images—pathway and shelter—reflect the tension in ritualization between the verb and the noun" (Driver, 16). A good example of this image at work in some people's lives is the practice of nighttime prayer, or a bedtime story.

Daily ritualizing behaviors help us touch mystery without being overwhelmed by it. They offer us different hierarchical levels of meaning and gradually help us to see through the mirror of the ordinary into the extraordinary or the mystical. In times of grief, for example, rituals help us to maneuver the dangerous path of loss, fear, and loneliness. They will almost certainly change in form according to the need and seasons of our life. Participants might recognize that certain aspects of a particular ritual no longer fit the context or perspective of their life, so they reconfigure the ritual to speak to the evolving need. Tom Driver, professor of theology and culture at Union Theological Seminary, explains:

> Whereas received rituals guide practitioners along known paths, ritualizings create pathways in response to new moral obligations. In times of crisis when received wisdom is inadequate to the new situation, groping may come to our aid. Confronting radically new dangers and moral challenges, we need to shift our magic circles and redefine the sacred. (50)

Since human beings are ritualizing creatures, it should come as no surprise that there are various modes or layers of ritual expression. These layers have ascending levels of importance and meaning. We choose them, consciously or unconsciously, to express the inexpressible and to help us manage or control our reality. These expressions include, but are not limited to, the following: rituals, ceremonies, ritualizing behaviors, customs, habits, and routines.

Ceremonies differ from rituals in that they *mark times of accomplishment* or completion. They are actions performed with formality, but lack any deep significance, force, or effect. Often they are elaborate acts or gestures of politeness or etiquette, which cover over the lack of any real interior importance. By design, ceremonies are not meant to be transformative. They are often, though not always, secular in nature, and have a large audience. Weddings and graduations, retirement, military, graveside, and political cere-monies fall into this category. Although a particular individual in a ceremony or a member of the subject's family (e.g., the wedding couple, the retiree, the graduate, or the political candidate) may experience the ceremony as a transforming ritual, the audience generally experiences it as a ceremony. There are exceptions of course. In authentic ritual, there is no audience, only participants.

In the popular culture, many people confuse ritual and ceremony, which can cause mistrust of the work of trans-forming words and actions. *Ceremonies* typically use volumes of words with little real action or depth, but *rituals* are authenticated by the way they *include the shadow*, the unat-tractive side of life. This inclusion of the shadow is what facilitates the *transformative work* of ritual. Ritual expression often acknowledges this dark aspect of our humanity. If the shadow is not present, then the event is a ceremony and not a ritual.

Ritualizing behavior, on the other hand, helps us *face the chaos of life* through a specific and simple *ordered action*, such as cleaning out a closet, weeding the garden, or paint-ing a room, while in the midst of an emotional crisis. The experience of ordering a selected part of our life helps create an interior sense of balance in the psyche that helps us to move in a healthier way through the present crisis. Since we are hardwired for ritual expression, ritualizations can also be manifested in such low-grade forms as obsessions, addic-tions, compulsions, and neurotic behavior. The difference is that there is no liberating aspect to these forms. Rather than helping us face the chaos of life, these actions are, in reality, escapes from the legitimate suffering necessary to work through the encoded message.

Routines are also often confused with rituals. A routine is a habitual method of performance or *established procedure* (e.g., beginning the day with a cup of coffee or morning shower) completed without much insight or awareness that might give us a *measure of comfort.*

Habits are *repetitive behavior patterns* that help us move more smoothly through life (e.g., a cigarette or drink after dinner). I know many women who have the habit of going shopping when they are stressed. They often refer to it as "therapy."

When we do not consciously integrate the shadow into our lives, we unconsciously set up a parallel ritual system, with its own modes of expression, that is unmanaged. In this case, reality becomes the ritual. This is seen in some accidents, psychosomatic illnesses, and self-negating behavior. Grasping the concept of the shadow is difficult but necessary work if we are to secure the fullness of our humanity. The shadow material is composed of all the thoughts, attitudes, and emotions (positive and negative) that are not acceptable for the individual or collective psyche to hold at a conscious level. These aspects can be noble qualities, such as creativity or childlikeness, or the baser qualities of anger or hatred. The decision of what to place in our shadow is determined by family and cultural influences. This decision-making process often occurs subconsciously. The soulful work of reclaiming the shadow and bringing its treasure to consciousness is courageous work. This moral imperative is the stuff of creating our own happiness. The fate of the soul is the fate of the social order in that when the shadow is repressed or denied, it can be become violent and dangerous; when it is wisely integrated, however, it often becomes golden and powerful. The shadow is in the service of the whole person or community. It yearns to be consciously acknowledged or expressed. William Blake, the nineteenth-century poet, described this process brilliantly with his image of going to hell for energy and to heaven for form, and learning to marry the two.

Psychoanalyst C. G. Jung expanded Freud's concept of the shadow by offering a clearer understanding of how engagement with the shadow could lead to individuation:

> Everyone carries a shadow, and the less it is embodied in the individual's conscious life, the blacker and denser it is. If an inferiority is conscious, one always has a chance to correct it. Furthermore, it is constantly in contact with other interests, so that it is continually subjected to modifications. But if it is repressed and isolated from consciousness, it never gets corrected, and is liable to burst forth suddenly in a moment of unawareness. (*CW*, 11:76)

This is where the danger lurks—when the shadow is out of relationship with the rest of our consciousness. Jung continues:

> If the repressed tendencies, the shadow as I call them, were obviously evil, there would be no problem whatever. But the shadow is merely somewhat inferior, primitive, unadapted, and awkward; not wholly bad. It even contains childish or primitive qualities which would in a way vitalize and embellish human existence, but— convention forbids! (*CW*, 11:78)

Living with the inferior, primitive, or unadapted aspects of our humanity is a challenging task calling for great awareness and humility. The civilizing process of inculturation sorts out which characteristics belong to the ego or to the shadow. Robert Johnson points out: "The unconscious cannot tell the difference between a 'real' act and a symbolic

one. This means that we can aspire to beauty and goodness—and pay out that darkness in a symbolic way" *Owning
Your Own Shadow* (21). This is a powerful statement, and it
has immense ramifications for living a symbolic life. Living
symbolically can prevent individuals or communities from
feeling trapped by their evil inclinations or repetitive behav-
ioral tendencies.

Johnson offers a simple example of how this dilemma
can be ritually expressed in a matter of minutes. Speaking of
two women friends of C. G. Jung, he points out:

> Dr. Marie-Louise von Franz and Barbara Hannah,
> who shared a household in Kusnacht, Switzerland,
> had the custom of requiring whoever had had
> some especially good fortune, to carry out the
> garbage for the week. This is a simple but power-
> ful act. Symbolically speaking, they were playing
> out the shadow side of something positive.
> (*Owning Your Own Shadow*, 19)

This is a credible approach, once it is accepted that the
soul cannot tell the difference between a ritual and reality.
The proposition might be put that this lack of distinction
could undermine the value of ritual. However, in my own
experience as a ritual practitioner, and in the experience of
many other Western ritual practitioners, including Richard
Rohr, Robert Johnson, and the African Malidoma Somé, it is
a valid one.

Something as seemingly insignificant as consciously
taking out the trash for a week can be a ritual of ego-deflation
that experientially reminds us of our limitations in the face
of the ego-inflating sense of success. This small conscious ritual, which honors the shadow, if practiced confidently and
intentionally, is useful in bringing a healthy balance to our
conscious life. We are reminded, through experience, of the

full continuum of our humanity—both the light and dark aspects of our personhood. Holding both truths in tension simultaneously is the work of the poet, the artist, and, indeed, the mature human being.

Failure to attend to the shadow side of reality can create needless neurotic suffering and chaos. Often neurosis becomes the replacement for the legitimate work of individuation. As Johnson notes:

> To refuse the dark side of one's nature is to store up or accumulate the darkness; this is later expressed as a black mood, psychosomatic illness, or unconsciously inspired accidents. We are presently dealing with the accumulation of a whole society that has worshipped its light side and refused the dark, and this residue appears as war, economic chaos, strikes, racial intolerance. The front page of any newspaper hurls the collective shadow at us. (*Owning Your Own Shadow*, 26)

Careful attention to both the light and dark sides of the human psyche can benefit not only the individual but also society by infusing and directing this creative energy. To give some dignity to this human internal conflict, or to violence in general, we could ritually express the turmoil through art, music, or crafts. This point is illustrated in an interesting exchange I experienced some years ago with an adolescent client. The presenting issue was inappropriate violent behavior on the part of the client toward his classmates. During one of our sessions, I asked him what he did when he became angry, and he informed me that he beat up people. "Is there anything else that you do?" I asked. "Yes," he said quietly, "I like to draw." I affirmed this choice and asked if he would show me samples of his artwork. The next week, he arrived with some powerfully expressive works of art. I asked him if he had shown these to his teacher, as she was the one who had lodged the original complaint that sent him to counseling. "Yes," he said, "but she didn't like the art because it was too violent, so she told me to stop it." Consequently, the only alternative the boy had in his coping skills was to lash out physically. His size and intellectual capacity made brutality an easy choice. At the end of our sessions, I presented him with a gift of art supplies, encouraging him to draw whenever he became angry. I never heard another complaint about him.

This is a further example of Johnson's argument that "the psyche is unaware of the difference between an outer act and an interior one. Our shadow qualities are lived out equally well—from the viewpoint of Self—either way. Culture can only function if we live out the unwanted elements symbolically" (*Owning Your Own Shadow*, 52).

The language of the soul is symbolic and metaphorical—hence the confusion in trying to incorporate this confluence of outer and inner modes into culturally appropriate behavior. One type of behavior may be correct on one level of reality but extremely dangerous on another. For example, suicide is literally an extreme form of self-destruction. As archetypal psychologist James Hillman says: "Because suicide is a way of entering death and because the problem of entering death releases the most profound fantasies of the human soul, to understand a suicide we need to know what mythic fantasy is being enacted" (*Suicide and the Soul*, 51). This perspective means paying attention to the *meaning* of the facts and circumstances of one's life, and not just the facts themselves. The necessity of dying to one's egocentric self, when translated into symbolic language, can be very liberating and life giving. Death, in reality or in imagination, can be an invitation to transformation or change as posited by Hillman:

[T]he soul needs the death experience. This can come about through various modes....Suicide is but one of the modes; some others are: depression, collapse, trance, isolation, intoxication and exaltation, failure, psychosis, dissociation, amnesia, denial, pain, and torture. These states can be expressed symbolically or concretely. *The mode of psychological experience seems not to matter to the soul providing it has the experience.* (83)

Sadly, many individuals, in their despair and haste to resolve the inner ambivalence, turn to the parallel shadow ritual of a literal suicide rather than a symbolic death. "Suicide is the attempt to move from one realm to another by force through death" (Hillman, 68). It is a means of truncating the agonizing struggle of the psyche with the paradox of contradictions in one's life. There are many complex anthropological reasons for such a phenomenon. How much healthier we would be if we had a richer ceremonial and ritual life to express our emotions!

The challenge of facing and integrating our shadow side pales when compared to the daunting task that any society faces in confronting and transforming the societal shadow for the good of all. Johnson extrapolates this concept: "All healthy societies have a rich ceremonial life. Less healthy ones rely on unconscious expressions: war, violence, psychosomatic illness, neurotic suffering, and accidents are very low-grade ways of living out the shadow. Ceremony and ritual are a far more intelligent means of accomplishing the same thing" (*Owning Your Own Shadow*, 52–53).

Without a full ceremonial and ritual life, society begins to decay. Symbolic containers that once reverently held the dark mysteries and struggles of people are shattered in the contemporary marketplace, where speed and efficiency are the new gods to be worshipped. The profane mentality of consumerism has invaded the sacred space of ritual and transformed it into a cookie-cutter response to life—one size fits all. Rather than carefully planning and executing unique rituals and ceremonies for specific persons and situations, contemporary society has generally co-opted old, outdated traditions and replaced rituals with glamorous ceremonies. We have become an entertainment culture at the price of losing our tradition of wisdom and transformation.

Questions for Personal Reflection:

- Have I ever participated in a failed ritual? What was the effect on me?
- What are some ways that my shadow has manifested itself in my life?
- How might the integration of shadow into a ritual expression help me live a more energetic, happier life?

Questions for Pastoral Leaders:

- How might we train others to live a more conscious life in a symbolic manner?
- What rituals can we create to assist others in problem-solving situations? How can we help parishioners when rituals have gone awry?
- In what ways can we bring about greater integration of the shadow aspects of our individual and community lives?

Tips for Pastoral Leaders:

- A failed ritual is not the end of the story. This chapter offers you insights into why failure is possible and gives a solid grounding for continuing the work of transformation and healing.
- Study other material on shadow work (see the Bibliography for recommendations).
- Therapy can be very helpful to hurting individuals, especially if it includes embodied practices. Indeed, we can assist people who are trapped in negative, repetitive behavior patterns (e.g., addictions, obsessions, compulsions, and neuroses).

9

Life Transformed:
It's a Whole New World

THE REGULAR PRACTICE and use of rituals can lead us into greater psychological health, at a personal as well as a societal level. In the lives of individuals, as well as in the public sector, rituals can assist in the work of individuation and communal responsibility. In the past, religion fulfilled the role, offering a cohesive sense of order and a mode of expression of the yearnings of the human soul. Unfortunately, historical realities have greatly diluted the effects of healthy religion in our society, leaving us with a dualistic split between material and spiritual reality. Such a split is manifested by a dramatic increase in violence at every level of society. What would happen if we were to reclaim the wisdom of ritual making on both the personal and communal levels of our culture, and revision this work for a happier people and a healthier society? I believe we would gradually transform the world.

Ritual does not guarantee transformation; rather, it offers the possibility of a new, changed life. What would transformation look like? Transformation is unique for each person; it is about becoming whole or individuated. It is about gradually growing into the fullness of our humanity in peace and happiness. A deepening and strengthening of such qualities as compassion, gentleness, truth speaking, inner harmony, courage, equanimity, and right relationship are powerful signs of a life transformed. These qualities are then available to be shared in our social circles, rippling out into the culture at large. The personal is a doorway into the universal, and the universal is the container of everything personal. To maintain the effects of this transformation, we need to be vigilant and disciplined in our regular use of ritual practice, carefully supporting that practice with different modes of ritualizing behavior.

I have explained that human beings are ritual-making and ritualizing creatures, who have at their disposal various modes of ritual expression. These layers of ritual expression help bring order and direction to our lives, especially in times of transition and turmoil. Let me summarize the most important points to remember for sound ritual practice, leading to transformation:

- Authentic rituals are transformative while ceremonies mark times of accomplishment or completion. Ritualizing behaviors occur in order to create order in a chaotic world, while routines are established procedures that bestow internal comfort on the practitioner. Habits are patterns of behavior that assist individuals to move smoothly through life.
- In the popular culture, rituals and ceremonies are often confused and misnamed. There is a significant difference between the two, as is illustrated by the following table:

Rituals	Ceremonies
• focused attention	* diffused attention
• liminal space/time	* literal space/time
• few symbols	* many symbols
• few words	* many words (e.g., speeches)
• embodied action (involvement)	* dramatic action (for show)

- engage the shadow   * function for comfort
  (polarities)
- witnessing community * audience

- Liminal space/time and the incorporation of the human shadow into ritual performance are constitutive elements of transformative ritual. Unless the shadow material of human beings becomes consciously integrated in some form or another, it will create an unconscious parallel ritual system as a means of self or communal expression.
- Rituals can give direction and meaning to the life journey of human beings, and therefore can be experienced as an ongoing intimate part of our developmental process. Rituals assist us in living consciously and purposefully. This form of embodied knowing can lead us into maturity and a measure of happiness throughout the challenges and transitions of life.
- Rituals have several functions in the overall dynamic of human life:

  - the enrichment of community
  - the ordering of one's life
  - the bridging of ego consciousness and the unconscious
  - the facilitation of developmental change and transition

These functions serve to enhance human well-being. Rituals can also assist us in negotiating the losses and "stuck places" in life.

- Following the work of Arnold van Gennep and Mircea Eliade, I have shown there are four steps to effective ritual enactment:
  - **Preparation:** the message to the soul that something significant is about to happen

- **Separation:** the public declaration that this is important work, and thus the individual must be "set apart" for a while
- **Ritual action:** the summary work in symbolic form and expression
- **Reincorporation:** the affirmation and confirmation of the participants by the witnessing community
- In addition, building on the work of Victor Turner, Ronald Grimes, Roy Rappaport, and C. G. Jung, I believe that rituals need the following dimensions or characteristics to be effective:
  - mindful preparation
  - conscious focused participation and attention
  - liminal space and time
  - multivocal symbol(s)
  - performative words
  - dramatic embodied action
  - engagement of the shadow and/or inner polarities
  - a witnessing community
- Rituals must respect and honor the context and the level of maturity of the participants, so that there is a free, uninhibited engagement with the ritual process; otherwise, the ritual may become abusive. Ritual should always be at the service of the well-being of the individual and the community and should never be used as a vehicle for mandatory participation or change.
- Cosmologically, rituals can offer a clearer connection with the universe and give meaning to one's life. Anthropologically and sociologically, rituals support communal relationships and social identity. Psychologically, rituals serve to offer an inner cohesion and expression of an internal dynamic. Therapeutically, rituals can be healing and reconciling aspects of individual and communal nurture. Spiritually, rituals can offer the possibility of broad-

ening one's soul understanding and relationship to the Divine.

Herein lies the transformation of lives.

For all the reasons outlined above, I am convinced that human beings should regularly and consciously enter into the many layers, aspects, and expressions of ritual, ceremony, ritualizing behavior, and meaningful routines and habits as an ongoing means of enhancing our lives and strengthening the overall happiness quotient within the human community and the cosmos.

Think of what our life would look like if we entered into a regular conscious practice of ritual making and ritualizing behavior. This discipline could assist us to live more happily and enthusiastically, with less fear and anxiety. Ritual making is a way of seeing and believing that cuts across religious and cultural boundaries to bring about greater harmony and unity within and between persons and communities. In effect, the regular use of rituals is a way of dying to egocentricity and rising to new life (John 12:24). This is the core message of the Christ event. Christ's redemptive work takes place through his living and dying, which is confirmed in the resurrection. The death–resurrection cycle is a lengthy ritual event that focuses on the symbol of the cross and the empty tomb. Christ engages the shadow of humanity via these historical symbols and courageously holds the shadow up for all to see. He transforms it in the transhistorical and transgeographical location of Calvary. His words, "It is finished" (John 19:30), telegraph to the cosmos that something new and creative has been launched. Darkness has been transformed by the light of consciousness. This action is confirmed by Christ's words during the resurrection event: "Peace be with you" (John 20:21) and "Receive the Holy Spirit" (John 20:22). There was no call for revenge or further violence. Instead, a different greeting and command are given to his followers and to the world: "As the Father has sent me, so I send you" (John 20:21). This greeting is a reminder to all of us of our inner essence and power—that God dwells in us, and when we live out our authentic humanity, we are most like God.

Let me conclude with a story: Several years ago, I was a member of a team of qualified professional men who worked with a group of youth at risk. We led the boys through an initiation experience that included a two-week canoeing expedition, several outdoor experiences, rituals, and discussions. It was an intense introduction into the adult world of responsibility and interdependence. Each boy faced his own struggles and challenges. The final ritual consisted of a sweat lodge experience in the Native American tradition, in which the boys shared a powerful bonding ritual. At the conclusion of this difficult and challenging process, Ralph, a thirteen-year-old marijuana addict, came to me and with deep sincerity said, "That was the best experience I have ever had in my life." Ralph had experienced the mystical, the really Real, and he no longer wanted the false or counterfeit experience of drugs. He no longer needed to lash out at others, since he had experienced an interior harmony. Ralph knew unitive bliss. The shackles of his past were broken; like Christ, he could say: "It is finished." Like Christ, he could enter a new life with peace and a clearer realization of his own power. Ralph could now hear and heed the call to be truly human and happy. He had crossed over into a completely new world, a new way of seeing and experiencing life. He and we who similarly yearn for transformation have the invitation to live out our lives in this sacred way of seeing anew with regular ritual and ritualizing practices.

It's a whole new world.

Questions for Personal Reflection:

- How can I transform my worldview through regular ritual practice and conscious ritualizing behavior? How can I broaden my ritual repertoire?
- How might I introduce these concepts into my relationships?
- In what other ways do I care for, or attend to, the needs of my soul?

Questions for Pastoral Leaders:

- How might we introduce these concepts into parish life and/or the parish school?
- In what other practical ways might we encourage active care for the souls of our people beyond familiar and traditional prayer practices?

Tips for Pastoral Leaders:

- Children are very open to the imaginal world and thus to ritual practice. Begin by teaching children how to support and strengthen their interior life through regular ritual practice.
- Consider working with adolescents on an initiation process.
- Create milestone rituals for families to use.
- Offer a midlife retreat where rituals of endings and beginnings can be celebrated.
- Teach people how to ritually prepare for death.

Appendix A

Liminality Contrasted with Status System

Transition / State
Totality / Partiality
Homogeneity / Heterogeneity
Communitas / Structure
Equality / Inequality
Anonymity / Systems of nomenclature
Absence of property / Property
Absence of status / Status
Nakedness or uniform clothing / Distinctions of
  clothing
Sexual continence / Sexuality
Minimization of sex distinctions / Maximization
  of sex distinctions
Absence of rank / Distinctions of rank
Humility / Just pride of position
Disregard for personal appearance / Care for
  personal appearance
No distinctions of wealth / Distinctions of wealth
Unselfishness / Selfishness
Total obedience / Obedience only to superior rank
Sacredness / Secularity
Sacred instruction / Technical knowledge

Silence / Speech
Suspension of kinship rights and obligations /
    Intermittent reference to mystical powers
Foolishness / Sagacity
Simplicity / Complexity
Acceptance of pain and suffering / Avoidance of
    pain and suffering
Heteronomy / Degrees of autonomy

(Turner, *The Ritual Process*, 106–7)

Appendix B

Types of Infelicitous Performances

- Misfire (act purported but void)
  - Misinvocation (act disallowed)
  - Nonplay (lack of accepted conventional procedure)
  - Misapplication (inappropriate persons or circumstances)
  - Misexecutions (act vitiated)
  - Flaw (incorrect, vague, or inexplicit formula)
  - Hitch (incomplete procedure)
- Abuse (act professed but hollow)
  - Insincerity (lack of requisite feelings, thoughts, or intentions)
  - Breach (failure to follow through)
  - "Gloss" (procedures used to cover up problems)
  - "Flop" (failure to produce appropriate mood or atmosphere)
- "Ineffectuality" (act fails to precipitate anticipated empirical change)
- "Violation" (act effective but demeaning)
- "Contagion" (act leaps beyond proper boundaries)
- "Opacity" (act unrecognizable or unintelligible)
- "Defeat" (act discredits or invalidates acts of others)

- "Omission" (act not performed)
- "Misframe" (genre of act misconstrued)

(J. L. Austin, in Grimes, "Ritual Criticism and Infelicitous Performances," *Readings in Ritual Studies*, 288)

Appendix C

Evaluation of Ritual— CASES Critique Method

Content

1= Outstanding, 3= Effective,
5= In need of significant improvement

- Community: Invites all participants into a shared experience
  1_____3_____5
  Comment:

- Action: Perceptible moment when the symbol is incarnated
  1_____ 3_____5
  Comment:

- Symbol: Clear physical element that unifies the experience
  1_____ 3_____5
  Comment:

- Environment: Liminal space is delineated before and after ritual
  1_____ 3_____5
  Comment:

- Story: The larger story of creation is represented

  1_____3 _____5
  Comment:

Transformative Effect
1= Outstanding, 3= Effective,
5= In need of significant improvement

- Community: Moves participants from a private to communal experience
  1_____3_____5
  Comments:

- Action: Engages participation rather than observation
  1_____3_____5
  Comment:

- Symbol: The ordinary becomes a metaphor for the divine
  1_____3_____5
  Comment:

- Environment: A sense of authentic mystery is created
  1_____3_____5
  Comment:

- Story: Participants are left with an invitation to apply the lesson to life

  1_____3_____5
  Comment:

_____

Evaluator
(Richard Groves, **Sacred Art of Living Center**)

Bibliography

Anderson, Herbert, and Edward Foley. *Mighty Stories, Dangerous Rituals: Weaving Together the Human and the Divine*. San Francisco: Jossey-Bass, 1998.

Clarke, James J. *Ritual: A Mythic Means of Personal and Social Transformation*. Carpinteria, CA: Pacifica Graduate Institute, 2008.

Deal, Terrence E., and Allan A. Kennedy. *Corporate Cultures: The Rites and Rituals of Corporate Life*. Reading, MA: Addison-Wesley, 1982.

Driver, Tom F. *Liberating Rites: Understanding the Transformative Power of Ritual*. Boulder, CO: Westview Press, 1998.

Eliade, Mircea. *Myth and Reality*. New York: Harper and Row, 1963.

———. *Rites and Symbols of Initiation: The Mysteries of Birth and Rebirth*. New York: Harper and Row, 1958.

———. *Rites and Symbols of Initiation: The Mysteries of Birth and Rebirth*. Translated by Willard R. Trask. Putnam, CT: Spring, 1994.

———. *The Sacred and the Profane: The Nature of Religion*. New York: Harper and Row, 1961.

Feinstein, David, and Peg Elliott Mayo. *How We Can Turn Loss and the Fear of Death into an Affirmation of Life*. San Francisco: Harper, 1990.

Gordon, R. *Dying and Creating a Search for Meaning*. London: The Library of Analytical Psychology, 1978.

Granach, Stephen M. *Ceremonial Rites of Passage for Adolescent Boys: Essential Components for Contemporary Initiations.* Long Beach, CA: California State University at Long Beach, 2001.

Grillo, Laura. Class notes, Pacifica Graduate Institute, 2005.

Grimes, Ronald L. *Beginnings in Ritual Studies.* Rev. ed., Columbia, SC: University of South Carolina Press, 1990.

————. *Deeply into the Bone: Re-Inventing Rites of Passage.* Berkeley, CA: University of California Press, 2000.

————. *Marrying and Burying: Rites of Passage in a Man's Life.* Boulder, CO: Westview Press, 1995.

————. *Reading, Writing and Ritualizing: Ritual in Fictive, Liturgical and Public Places.* Washington, DC: Pastoral Press, 1993.

————. *Readings in Ritual Studies.* Upper Saddle River, NJ: Prentice Hall, 1996.

————. *Rite Out of Place: Ritual Media and the Arts.* New York: Oxford University Press, 2006.

Groves, Richard. Class notes. Albuquerque, NM. February 2006.

Hillman, James. *Suicide and the Soul.* 2nd ed. Woodstock, CT: Spring, 1997.

Imber-Black, Evan, and Janine Roberts. *Rituals for Our Times: Celebrating, Healing, and Changing Our Lives and Our Relationships.* Northvale, NJ: Jason Aronson, 1998.

Irani, George Emile. "Apologies and Reconciliation: Middle Eastern Rituals." In Eleazar Barkan and Alexander Karn, eds. *Taking Wrongs Seriously: Apologies and Reconciliation.* Palo Alto, CA: Stanford University Press, 2006.

Johnson, Robert A. *Owning Your Own Shadow: Understanding the Dark Side of the Psyche.* San Francisco: Harper, 1991.

————. *Transformation: Understanding the Three Levels of Masculine Consciousness.* San Francisco: Harper, 1991.

Jung, C. G. *Collected Works.* Vol. 11. *Psychology and Religion:*

West and East. 2nd ed. Bollingen. Series XX. Princeton, NJ: Princeton University Press, 1958.

Levinson, Daniel J., ed. *The Seasons of a Man's Life*. New York: Ballantine Books, 1978.

Mahdi, Louise Carus, Nancy Gever Christopher, and Michael Meade, eds. *Crossroads: The Quest for Contemporary Rites of Passage*. Chicago, IL: Open Court, 1996.

Mahdi, Louise Carus, Steven Foster, and Meredith Little, eds. *Betwixt and Between: Patterns of Masculine and Feminine Initiation*. LaSalle, IL: Open Court, 1987.

Meade, Michael. *Men and the Water of Life: Initiation and the Tempering of Men*. San Francisco: Harper, 1993.

Merton, Thomas. "Symbolism: Communication or Communion?" *Mountain Path*. October 1966: 339–48.

Price, J. "New Divorce Rituals." *Family Therapy Networker* 13.4 (1989): 45.

Raphael, Ray. *The Men from the Boys: Rites of Passage in Male America*. Lincoln and London: University of Nebraska Press, 1988.

Rappaport, Roy A. *Ritual and Religion in the Making of Humanity*. Cambridge, UK: Cambridge University Press, 1999.

Rilke, Rainer Maria. *Letters to a Young Poet: Revised Edition*. Translated by M. D. Herter. New York: W. W. Norton, 1934.

Rohr, Richard. *Adam's Return: The Five Promises of Male Initiation*. New York: Crossroad, 2004.

———. *The Wild Man's Journey: Reflections on Male Spirituality*. Rev. ed. Cincinnati, OH: St. Anthony Messenger Press, 1996.

Sanford, John A. *Healing and Wholeness*. New York: Paulist Press, 1977.

Sanford, John A., and George Lough. *What Men Are Like: The Psychology of Men, for Men and the Women Who Live with Them*. New York: Paulist Press, 1988.

Somé, Malidoma Patrice. *Ritual: Power, Healing, and Community*. New York: Penguin Compass, 1993.

Stein, Murray. *In Midlife: A Jungian Perspective*. Putnam, CT: Spring, 1983.

Stevenson, K. *To Join Together: The Rite of Marriage*. New York: Pueblo, 1987.

Turner, Victor. "Betwixt and Between: The Criminal Period in Rites of Passage." In *Betwixt and Between: Patterns of Masculine and Feminine Initiation*. Eds. Louise Carus Mahdi, Steven Foster, and Meredith Little. LaSalle, IL: Open Court, 1987. 3–19.

———. *The Ritual Process: Structure and Anti-Structure*. New York: Aldine De Gruyter, 1997.

Van der Hart, Onno. *Coping with Loss: Psychotherapeutic Use of Leave-Taking Rituals*. New York: Irvington, 1988.

Van Gennep, Arnold. *The Rites of Passage*. Translated by Monika B. Vizedom and Gabrielle L. Caffee. Chicago: University of Chicago Press, 1960.

Wall, Kathleen, and Gary Ferguson. *Rites of Passage: Celebrating Life's Changes*. Hillsboro, OR: Beyond Words, 1998.